The Short Guide Series

UNDER THE EDITORSHIP OF

Sylvan Barnet
Marcia Stubbs

From Steven Spielberg's *Close Encounters of the Third Kind*

A Short Guide
to Writing
about Film

A Short Guide to Writing about Film

TIMOTHY CORRIGAN

Temple University

HarperCollins*CollegePublishers*

Acquisitions Editor: Patricia Rossi
Project Editor: Robert Ginsberg
Design Supervisor: Heather A. Ziegler
Cover Design: Wendy Ann Fredericks
Cover Photo: © 1992 New Line Productions, Inc. All rights reserved.
  Photo by Lori Sebastian. Photo appears courtesy of New Line Cinema
  Corporation.
Production Manager/Assistant: Willie Lane/Sunaina Sehwani
Compositor: KP Company
Printer and Binder: R. R. Donnelly & Sons Company
Cover Printer: The Lehigh Press, Inc.

For permission to use copyrighted material, grateful acknowledgment is made to the copyright holders on pp. 183–184, which are hereby made part of this copyright page.

A Short Guide to Writing about Film, Second Edition
Copyright © 1994 by Timothy J. Corrigan

Library of Congress Cataloging-in-Publication Data

Corrigan, Timothy.
    A short guide to writing about film / Timothy Corrigan.
        p.   cm. — (The Short guide series)
    Includes bibliographical references and index.
    ISBN 0-673-52299-7
    1. Film criticism — Study and teaching.   I. Title.
  PN1995.C66   1994
  791.43'028'092273 — dc20
[B]
                                                    93-21631
                                                    CIP

93 94 95 96   9 8 7 6 5 4 3 2 1

For David Cook

Contents

Preface

Those who teach film rarely have time to discuss writing about film. Most instructors are busy presenting films and books about those films, and the usual presumption they are forced to make is that students know how to put what they see and think into a comprehensible written form. As common and forgivable as that presumption may be, it is less reliable today than ever before. Instructors must increasingly puzzle over and bemoan those enthusiastic students who seem to know so much and who are brimming with things to say about the movies, but who write confused and disappointing papers.

One way to avoid this problem is to rely on examinations that elicit short answers. Yet, as useful and as necessary as this method is, especially with large lecture courses in film history, it sidesteps several beneficial demands that the critical essay makes, demands that lead to real differences in the quality of a student's thinking. An essay forces a student to use special skills: to generate and focus original ideas; to organize, sustain, and support those ideas until they are fully developed; to fine-tune perceptions by revising the language used to describe them; to employ proper grammar and syntax as part of a convincing presentation of an argument; and to make use of the opinions of others through intelligent research.

Writing about films is one of the most sophisticated ways to respond to them. To elicit scope, originality, and rigor in a student's thinking, an instructor, I believe, needs to guide that student through the mechanics of the essay form. This book hopes to be that guide.

The aim of this book is threefold: to save time for instructors of film who, in presenting the complexities of the art and industry of film are hard put to deal with the writing problems of students; to lessen students' anxiety about writing by clarifying points that many instructors mistakenly presume students already know; and, in doing this, to make for more enjoyable and articulate communication between the two. This book attempts to fill the gap between writing handbooks and film studies texts by distilling writing lessons as they apply specifically to film criticism. If it succeeds, everyone will be happier.

Although the emphasis here is on the analytical writing done in most film courses, the book can be used in many ways, with a variety of other texts, and by any professor who believes writing about film is part of learning abut film. It is, after all, a short book.

NOTE ON THE SECOND EDITION

The more I have taught courses in film studies, the more convinced I am, first, of how important good writing is to a sound critical engagement with film and, second, what an effective vehicle film studies is for eliciting good writing from students. During the last four years, my conversations with colleagues have seemed to support these notions, and I am grateful for the suggestions and comments I received from many individuals (especially Timothy Lyons) about where this book works well and where it might be improved. Indeed, enough in this book seems to work well so that I have not attempted a major overhaul. On the other hand, there were obvious errors that needed to be corrected, sources and examples which required updating, and certain additions which should further assist students. The passion for revision can of course be interminable, and I have tried to balance this urge with the knowledge that, especially in this case, a small book remains a better and more useful book.

My students at Temple University have been my best guides in revising this book. What they do not tell me bluntly, they say very clearly in the successes and failures of the essays they submit. I am grateful to them for this, as well as for not being too hard on a professor who has the audacity to teach his own book.

Two people have been unusually patient and helpful in reading the manuscript and urging changes: Marcia Stubbs and Sylvan Barnet. I am also grateful to the following for ideas, assistance, and encouragement: Cecilia Graham Corrigan, Marcia Ferguson, and the city of Tokyo, where much of this book was written.

The following reviewers of the first edition were very helpful: Austin Briggs, Hamilton College; David Cook, Emory University; Timothy J. Lyons, Emerson College; and James Schwoch, Northwestern University.

My special thanks this time to Anna — for the background.

TIMOTHY CORRIGAN

*A Short Guide
to Writing
about Film*

1

Writing About the Movies

WHY WRITE ABOUT MOVIES?

Commenting some years ago on his experience at the movies, the French writer Christian Metz described a challenge that still faces the student of movies today: we all understand the movies, but how do we explain them?

As a measure of that ease of understanding, notice the extent to which movies are a part of a cultural life that we generally take for granted. We all have films that we treasure and identify with, for their laughs, their thrills, or their haunting images of terror. Movie stars become cult figures and active politicians; Rambo is a household name; *Star Wars* (1977) is linked with a controversial military project; and *JFK* (1991) provokes a debate about John Kennedy's assassination that appears on television and in newspapers for months before and after the movie's release. In a sense, Erwin Panofsky's words of 1934 are probably truer today than ever: "If all the serious lyrical poets, composers, painters and sculptors were forced by law to stop their activities, a rather small fraction of the general public would become aware of the fact and a still smaller fraction would seriously regret it. If the same thing were to happen with the movies, the social consequences would be catastrophic." In short, publicly and privately, most of us have become so absorbed in movies that we rarely think about them — and less often, if at all, do we think of writing about them.

Normally we might argue that there is little reason to struggle to explain — and certainly not in writing — what we understand primarily as entertainment. Whether in a movie theater or watching late-night television, we usually watch films because we expect the kind of pleasure seldom associated with an inclination to pick up pen and paper. After seeing *Repo Man* (1984), we might chat briefly about certain characters, music, or scenes we particularly enjoyed or disliked, but we rarely want to offer a lengthy analysis of how the sets and music worked together. There is often an unspoken assumption that any kind of analysis might interfere with our enjoyment of the movies.

We are less reluctant to think analytically about other forms of entertainment. If, for instance, we watch a dance performance or a basketball game, we may easily and happily discuss some of the intricacies and complexities of those performances, realizing that our commentary adds to, rather than subtracts from, our enjoyment of an event. At these times, our understanding of and pleasure in experiencing the event are a product of the critical awareness that our discussion refines and elaborates on. The person who has no inclination or ability to reflect on or analyze basketball or dance may be entertained on some level, but the person who is able to activate a critical intelligence about the rules and possibilities involved experiences a more intricate kind of pleasure.

In fact, our ability to respond with some analytical awareness adds to our enjoyment. And, not surprisingly, the same is true of our enjoyment of the movies. Informed audiences often turn to read a review of a show they have seen the night before; many of us enjoy reading about movies we have not even seen. Analytical thinking and reading about an "entertainment" invigorate and enrich it and perhaps make the event itself more entertaining. Analytical writing about film offers the same promises and rewards. For example, when pressured to explain carefully his love of *Repo Man*, one student discovered that there were dimensions to his experience that he had not considered before. It was not simply the teenage hero of the movie who attracted him and his friends. He begins his expanded response:

> At first glance, Repo Man seems merely a teenage
> movie aimed at an audience that can identify with
> its hero and his struggles in society. While this is
> surely part of its attraction, Repo Man is exciting
> for less obvious reasons. Not only does Repo Man use
> some of the best new wave music, from musicians such
> as Iggy Pop, but it combines that music with a

```
visual style as humorous and dense as the most
interesting rock videos. What is most fascinating
for me is that this same rock-video style is found
in at least three other movies made about the same
time: Flashdance (1983), To Live and Die in L.A.
(1986), and Top Gun (1986).
```

If the movies inform many parts of our lives, we should be able to enjoy them in many ways, including the challenging pleasure of trying to think about, explain, and write about our experience at the movies. We go to the movies for many reasons: to think, not to think; to stare at them, to write about them. We may go to a movie to consume it like cotton candy; we may go to a film where that candy becomes food for the mind. As the fan of *Repo Man* found out, analyzing our response to a movie does not ruin our enjoyment of it. Writing about a film can allow us to enjoy it (and other films) in ways we were incapable of before. If watching and understanding is one of the pleasures of the movies, writing and explaining can be another exciting pleasure.

Let us keep in mind that writing about the movies is not so far from what most of us do already: when we leave a movie theater after two hours of enforced silence, most of us discuss or argue about a film. Although the difference between talking and writing about a subject is a crucial one, writing about a film is in one sense simply a more refined and measured kind of communication, this time with a reader. Our comments can be about the performance of an actor, the excitement elicited by specific scenes, or just common questions about what happened, why it happened, or why the film made the answers to these questions unclear.

Frequently these conversations evolve from searching for the right word or finding a satisfactory description of how a sequence developed: "I prefer Keaton to Chaplin because Keaton's funnier. . . . Well, I mean, he tells funnier . . . more complicated stories. . . ."; "I hated . . . no, felt unconvinced by the ending of *Grand Canyon* (1991)." While talking about movies, even very casually, we search for words to match what we saw and how we reacted to it. Writing about film is a careful and more calculated step beyond this first impulse to discuss what we have seen. Given this normal impulse, we can even enjoy talking and writing about

a movie that we didn't like. A friend of the writer who praised *Repo Man*
thus began her essay more negatively:

> <u>Repo Man</u> is a slick, rollicking movie, targeted
> at a teenage audience and full of wonderful gags and
> characters certain to please that audience. The
> visual style and music is like an extended rock
> video. Yet, that is exactly what is so disappointing
> about this earthy cartoon. It promises to be a
> refreshing and novel look at teenage anxiety, pre-
> sented through images teenagers know; instead it
> gives us a disconnected series of silly episodes
> without substance or meaning.

Maybe because two people can understand the same movie very
differently, trying to explain that understanding can be charged with all
the energy of a good conversation.

Perhaps more than most other arts and entertainments, the movies
frequently elicit a strong emotional or intellectual reaction. Often, however, the reason for our particular reaction to a movie remains unclear
until we have had the opportunity to think carefully about and articulate
what stimulated it. *Meet John Doe* (1941) might elicit a giddy nostalgia
ridiculously out of step with today's political complexities; a woman
viewer of *Kramer vs. Kramer* (1979) can find herself moved by the
melodramatic power of the film but may be uncomfortable with its
representation of women (specifically, the mother); most audiences of
Fellini's *8 1/2* (1963) will probably recognize the importance of the
opening sequence, in which a man floats from his car above a traffic jam,
but they may be hard put to explain quickly what it means in terms of the
story that follows. Analyzing our reactions to themes, characters, or
images like these can be a way not only of understanding a movie better,
but of understanding better how we view the world and the cultures we
live in. In the following three paragraphs, we can see how Geoffrey Nowell-
Smith turns his initial excitement about a scene in an Antonioni film into

an exploration of that particular scene and, implicitly, into a discussion of his admiration of the human complexity in Antonioni's films:

> There is one brief scene in *L'Avventura,* not on the face of it a very important one, which seems to me to epitomize perfectly everything that is most valid and original about Antonioni's form of cinema. It is the scene where Sandro and Claudia arrive by chance at a small village somewhere in the interior of Sicily. The village is strangely quiet. They walk around for a bit, call out. No reply, nothing. Gradually it dawns on them that the village is utterly deserted, uninhabited, perhaps never was inhabited. There is no one in the whole village but themselves, together and alone. Disturbed, they start to move away. For a moment the film hovers: the world is, so to speak, suspended for two seconds, perhaps more. Then suddenly the film plunges, and we cut to a close-up of Sandro and Claudia making love in a field — one of the most ecstatic moments in the history of the cinema, and one for which there has been apparently no formal preparation whatever. What exactly has happened?
>
> It is not the case that Sandro and Claudia have suddenly fallen in love, or suddenly discovered at that moment that they have been in love all along. Nor, at the other extreme, is theirs a panic reaction to a sudden fear of desolation and loneliness. Nor again is it a question of the man profiting from a moment of helplessness on the part of the woman in order to seduce her. Each of these explanations contains an aspect of the truth, but the whole truth is more complicated and ultimately escapes analysis. What precisely happened in that moment the spectator will never know, and it is doubtful if the characters really know for themselves. Claudia knows that Sandro is interested in her. By coming with him to the village she has already more or less committed herself, but the actual fatal decision is neither hers nor his. It comes, when it comes, impulsively: and its immediate cause, the stimulus which provokes the response, is the feeling of emptiness and need created by the sight of the deserted village. Just as her feelings (and his too for that matter) are neither purely romantic nor purely physical, so her choice, Antonioni is saying, is neither purely determined nor purely free. She chooses, certainly, but the significance of her choice escapes her, and in a sense also she could hardly have acted otherwise.

• • •

Where in this oppressive physical and social environment do the characters find any escape? How can they break out of the labyrinth which nature and other men and their own sensibilities have built up around them? Properly speaking there is no escape, nor should there be. Man is doomed to living in the world — this is to say no more than that he is doomed to exist. But the situation is not hopeless. There are moments of happiness in the films, which come, when they come, from being at peace with the physical environment, or with others, not in withdrawing from them. Claudia in *L'Avventura*, on the yacht and then on the island, is cut off, mentally, from the other people there, and gives herself over to undiluted enjoyment of her physical surroundings, until with Anna's disappearance even these surroundings seem to turn against her and aggravate rather than alleviate her pain. In *The Eclipse* Vittoria's happiest moment is during that miraculous scene at Verona when her sudden contentment seems to be distilled out of the simple sights and sounds of the airport: sun, the wind in the grass, the drone of an aeroplane, a juke-box. At such moments other people are only a drag — and yet the need for them exists. The desire to get away from oneself, away from other people, and the satisfaction this gives, arise only from the practical necessity for most of the time of being aware of oneself and of forming casual or durable relationships with other people. And the relationships too can be a source of fulfillment. No single trite or abstract formulation can catch the living essence of Antonioni's version of the human comedy. (Nichols 355, 363)

In this example, a single scene becomes the stimulus for the essay. The author probes and questions this scene: what exactly has happened, and what does it mean? His obvious satisfaction as a writer comes from analyzing this scene as if it were a mystery to be solved. In the process of his analysis, his original curiosity leads to broader readings of other Antonioni movies and finally to his discovery of a consolation in the disturbing predicament that first caught his eye. For this writer, the pleasure of following his curiosity leads to the larger pleasure of understanding more about life and happiness in modern times.

YOUR AUDIENCE AND THE AIMS OF FILM CRITICISM

Writing about film can serve one or several functions. It can help you

- understand your own response to a movie better
- convince others why you like or dislike a film
- explain or introduce something about a movie, a filmmaker, or a group of movies that your readers may not know
- make comparisons and contrasts between one movie and others, as a way of understanding them better

- make connections between a movie and other areas of culture in order to illuminate both the culture and the movies it produces

The purposes that become part of or central to your writing will sometimes depend entirely on your audience: an essay introducing a new movie, for example, will usually be written for an audience that has not seen the film. However, even when that purpose is decided independently — perhaps out of a personal interest in the relation between Spanish films and Spanish culture — what you write will always be shaped by your notion of your audience, and especially by what you presume those readers know or want to know.

If you think of writing as, in some ways, resembling conversation, you will see how the notion of an audience helps to shape what you say. If, for example, you are discussing an American movie, such as Robert Altman's *Nashville* (1975), with a non-American, both the way you make your point about the film and perhaps the point itself will be determined by what you believe that individual knows and wants to know about American culture and about the movie itself. (A non-American, for example, may need to be told what the city of Nashville and its music mean to Americans, while an American will need very little explanation.) Similarly, if I were discussing a film with someone who may not have seen it, I would probably describe that film with a general overview at first, summarizing the plot and themes as a way of convincing that person to see the film or not to see it. When, on the other hand, I am talking about a movie that a friend and I have both seen several times — such as *Wayne's World* (1991), I do not have to remind that person of the plot or of which actors played which parts. Just as our conversations about movies differ according to the individuals we are speaking with, the way we write about film, and even the function we choose, will vary depending on the audience we are writing for.

One schematic and traditional way to indicate the different audiences a writer might envision is to distinguish between a review, a theoretical essay, and a critical essay.

The Movie Review

The review is the type of film analysis most of us are chiefly familiar with, since it appears in almost every newspaper. Normally a review aims at the broadest possible audience, the general public with no special knowledge of film. Accordingly, its function is to introduce unknown films and to recommend or not recommend them. Because it presumes an audience that has not seen the movie it discusses, much of the essay is devoted to summarizing the plot or placing the film in some context (the director's other work, films of the same genre, etc.) that might help the reader understand it. Here, Vincent Canby's review introduces the readers of *The New York Times* to Terrence Malick's *Badlands* (1974):

> In Terrence Malick's cool, sometimes brilliant, always ferociously American film, "Badlands," which marks Malick's debut as a director, Kit and Holly take an all-American joyride across the upper Middle West, at the end of which more than half a dozen people have been shot to death by Kit, usually at point blank range. "Badlands" is the first feature by Mr. Malick, a 29-year-old former Rhodes Scholar and philosophy student whose only other film credit is as the author of the screenplay for the nicely idiosyncratic "Pocket Money." "Badlands" was inspired by the short, bloody saga of Charles Starkweather who, at age 19, in January, 1958, with the apparent cooperation of his 14-year-old girlfriend, Carol Fugate, went off on a murder spree that resulted in 10 victims. Starkweather was later executed in the electric chair and Miss Fugate given life imprisonment.
>
> "Badlands" inevitably invites comparisons with three other important American films — Arthur Penn's "Bonnie and Clyde" and Fritz Lang's "Fury" and "You Only Live Once" — but it has a very different vision of violence and death. Mr. Malick spends no great amount of time invoking Freud to explain the behavior of Kit and Holly, nor is there any Depression to be held ultimately responsible. Society is, if anything, benign. . . .
>
> "Badlands" is narrated by Holly in the flat, nasal accents of the Middle West and in the syntax of a story in True Romances. "Little did I realize," she tells us at the beginning of the film, "that what began in the alleys and by-ways of this small town would end in the Badlands of Montana." At the end, after half a dozen murders, she resolves never again to "tag around with the hell-bent type."
>
> Kit and Holly share with Bonnie and Clyde a fascination with their own press coverage, with their over-night fame ("The whole world was looking for us," says Holly, "for who knew where Kit would strike next?"), but a lack of passion differentiates them from the gaudy desperados of the thirties. Toward the end of their joyride, the bored Holly tells us she passed the time, as she sat in the front seat beside Kit, spelling out complete sentences with her tongue on the roof of her mouth.
>
> Mr. Malick tries not to romanticize his killers, and he is successful except for one sequence in which Kit and Holly hide out in a tree house as elaborate as anything the MGM art department ever designed for

Tarzan and Jane. Mr. Sheen and Miss Spacek are splendid as the self-absorbed, cruel, possibly psychotic children of our time, as are the members of the supporting cast, including Warren Oates as Holly's father.

One may legitimately debate the validity of Mr. Malick's vision, but not, I think, his immense talent. "Badlands" is a most important and exciting film. (40)

We can identify more than one function in this essay. Canby aims to convince his reader that *Badlands* is an important movie that is worth seeing, and he does this by introducing Malick and his credentials, by describing the plot and the historical background for that plot, by evaluating the acting, and by placing Malick's movie in the context of other films like it (specifically, *Bonnie and Clyde* [1967] and the two Fritz Lang movies). Equally important, however, is his clear sense of his audience: readers who probably know the popular *Bonnie and Clyde* but little about Malick and the background of *Badlands*. These are readers who have not yet seen the film and would like to know the outline of the story and a little about the characters and the actors.

The Theoretical Essay

The more theoretical essay — for instance, an essay on the relation of film and reality, on the political or ideological foundations of the movie industry, or on how film narrative is not like literary narrative — is at the other end of the spectrum. Such an essay often supposes that the reader possesses a great deal of knowledge about specific films, film history, and other writings about film. Its target audience, often advanced students or people who teach film, is usually very knowledgeable about the movies. Its aim is to explain some of the larger and more complex structures of the cinema and how we understand them. Note the changes in style, choice of words, and assumptions about the reader's knowledge that point to this writer's 1953 conception of her audience:

> Here is new art. For a few decades it seemed like nothing more than a new technical device in the sphere of drama, a new way of preserving and retailing dramatic performances. But today its development has already belied this assumption. The screen is not a stage, and what is created in the conception and realization of a film is not a play. It is too early to systematize any theory of this new art, but even in its present pristine state it exhibits quite beyond any doubt, I think — not only a new technique, but a new poetic mode. . . . (Langer 411)

Whereas Canby could use expressions suitable to a review, such as "gaudy desperados," "all-American joyride," and "important and exciting film," the phrases might seem out of place in an essay by the philosopher Susanne Langer. It is not that one style is more correct than the other; it is simply a question of audience. A novice to film studies might feel somewhat lost in Langer's comparatively accessible essay in film theory. The reason is that novices are not the audience that this writer supposes: she imagines an audience with experience in the study of history, aesthetics, and philosophy and some understanding of the debates about drama versus movies. The purpose of her essay is not difficult to see (she wants to convince the readers of the significance of film as an art), and the way she argues her point is understandable when we realize she is addressing an academic and intellectual community who, at the time, were suspicious about the status of the movies as an art form.

The Critical Essay

The critical essay usually expected in film courses falls between the theoretical essay and the movie review. The writer of this kind of essay presumes that his or her reader has seen or is at least familiar with the film under discussion, although that reader may not have thought extensively about it. This writer might therefore remind the reader of key themes and elements of the plot, but a lengthy retelling of the story of the film is neither needed nor tolerable. The focus of the essay is far more specific than that of a review, since the writer hopes to reveal subtleties or complexities that might have escaped viewers on a first or even a second viewing. Thus the essay might focus on a short sequence at the beginning of the film, or on a camera angle that becomes associated with a specific character. In the following excerpt, Brian Henderson also discusses *Badlands,* but, while Canby's audience was the reader of a large newspaper, Henderson's audience is more academic, similar to the one a student might address in a film course:

> Whatever their wishes, critics of Terrence Malick's *Badlands* (1974) have been drawn in to polemical dispute. Writers favorable to the film have defended it against those who called it a failure when it first appeared and against those who have ignored it since then. The issue has been further complicated, and polemics renewed, by the release in 1978 of Malick's *Days of Heaven.*

This is not a favorable background for the serious criticism of any work, still less for that open-ended exploration which a new and unstudied work invites. I believe *Badlands* is one of the most remarkable American films of the 1970s, but I have no interest here in addressing the arguments against it. I assume, at any rate, that the film will be seen and studied for a long time to come.

What is attempted here is a beginning analysis of *Badlands,* or perhaps several beginnings. I take an obvious point of departure: the film's voice-over narration by Holly — indeed only its first part, approximately the film's first sixteen minutes. This is, emphatically, just one approach to the film and not a privileged one. A consideration of Holly's narration opens up other topics and leads to other analyses, but any approach does this.

To treat Holly's narration as I wish to do it is necessary to say something in advance about the film's dramaturgy, acting style and use of language. These important topics deserve, needless to say, fuller treatment than my prefatory remarks provide.

Badlands' approach to character is undeniably modern. Kit and Holly are both blank and not blank, emotionless and filled with emotion, oblivious to their fates and caught up in them, committed to the trivial but aware — glancingly — of the essential. They are empty, hence constantly fill themselves up with useless objects, souvenirs, movie-magazine gossip; they pose tests for themselves and try on different make-up, clothes, attitudes, roles. This is an "existential" view of character, and it undoubtedly leads to contradictions by conventional standards. Thus Kit and Holly are in love, living only for the moments they spend together; but they play cards with boredom in the country and even find sex boring. Holly kids with her father and (almost) weeps when he dies, but runs away with his killer a few hours later. . . .

Every mode of cinema has a mode of dramaturgy distinctive to it and a corresponding distinctive acting or performance style. *Badlands,* which may represent a cinematic mode in and of itself, requires a special kind of acting to take its place within, but not upset, a very delicate balance of mise-en-scène, narrative, voice-over, music, etc. We must be able to look at Kit and Holly and to look through them sometimes alternately, sometimes simultaneously. This requires an acting style at once flat and flamboyant, realistic and theatrical. Our eyes must be on the characters even as we are paying attention to other things. Our attention is continually drawn toward the characters, and distracted away from them. Sheen and Spacek realize these requirements superbly, filling the film with their interesting sounds and motions but never resolving into anything, never substantializing, defining or "becoming" characters. Perhaps more correctly, their series of poses is readable as exactly that, or as eccentric character. As in Brecht, it is difficult to distinguish the acting style of the performers from the nature of the characters. (38-40)

Canby's and Henderson's essays are both positive responses to *Badlands,* and they share similar interests. They differ significantly, however, in aim and audience. At least as Henderson declares it, the purpose of his essay is not so much to convince his readers to like or dislike the film but to add to their understanding of it. He assumes that his readers will continue to see and study the movie and perhaps add to the academic debate about it. He also takes for granted that his audience knows the story, knows the characters, and is familiar with terms like "mise-en-scène"; he accordingly can choose very specific aspects of the film — Holly's narration and the acting style — to demonstrate his point that there are important innovations at work in *Badlands.* Finally, even in this section of the essay, one sees organization typical of a good critical argument: the writer begins by placing the film in the context of other critical and scholarly views, announces his aim, and then moves from an analysis of character and acting style to some general conclusions about how to understand this style.

For the student writer, the question of audience, highlighted in these three essays, is equally central to writing about film. Sometimes an instructor may give you an assignment aimed at a specific audience and testing your ability to address that audience: "Write a review of Abel Gance's *Napoleon* (1927) for the readers of *Time* magazine." More often your instructor will simply ask you to write a critical essay. Keep in mind that your audience in these cases is neither your instructor alone (who you might imagine can learn nothing from you) nor some large and unknown public in the streets (to whom you might be prone to tell the most obvious facts about a movie). Rather, envision your audience in most situations as your fellow students, individuals who have seen the movie and may know something about it but who have not studied it closely. This audience will probably not need to be told that "*The Wizard of Oz* is an old American film that has become a children's classic"; they may, however, be interested if you note that "*The Wizard of Oz* was directed by Victor Fleming, who the same year (1939) made *Gone with the Wind."* Likewise, few of your fellow viewers need to be told that "Ophul's *The Sorrow and the Pity* (1971) is a very long French movie about World War II"; they could, though, be fascinated by a detailed description of the opening shots.

OPINION AND EVALUATION

When you write about film, personal opinion and taste will necessarily become part of your argument. Some critics, for example, have a conscious or unconscious prejudice against foreign films. Others favor the work of a single director, such as John Huston or Alain Resnais. Still others, repelled by violence except when it is extremely stylized, dislike films such as *Texas Chainsaw Massacre* (1974) but defend the films of Brian De Palma. Even those essays that appear to be chiefly descriptive or analytical — biographical or historical writings or essays that aim to analyze objectively a sequence of shots — involve a certain amount of personal choice and evaluation. In some essays, factual description may be more prominent than evaluative judgments, but the differences are of degree, not kind. Most writing about film involves some personal opinion and evaluation.

No reader, of course, will be satisfied with a writer who uses his personal opinions to avoid or disguise a solid critical position. After watching Olivier's adaptation of Shakespeare's *Henry V* (1944), one student writes:

> Although I have not read that many Shakespeare plays, this is the first one I ever liked. The opening, I think, is the most interesting part and the section that first grabbed my attention, because, in my opinion, it literally transforms what I feel is a dry play into an exciting film and, at the same time, comments on the difference between drama and film. In those opening images, it seems to me that Olivier acknowledges the original stage-world of the drama and shows, I feel, how the movies can transcend dramatic limits. He makes the play much more alive for me.

Here the excess of "I"s and personal qualifiers weakens the point the writer wishes to make, and it is doubtful that idiosyncratic problems, such as the writer's limited experience with the Shakespeare plays, are of the faintest interest to any reader. However, removing all references to the writer's personal experience of the film only results in stiffer but equally unsure prose:

> The opening is the most interesting part of
> Henry V because it comments on the central differ-
> ence between drama and film. In these opening im-
> ages, Olivier acknowledges the original stage-world
> of the drama and shows how the movies can transcend
> those dramatic limits.

Somewhere in between these extremes, the writer will find the proper balance of personal experience and objective observation, judiciously integrating those personal experiences and feelings about the film that are probably also valid for other viewers:

> Even for the viewer uneasy with a Shakespeare play,
> Olivier's Henry V is an engaging experience. For me,
> the opening is the most interesting part and the
> section which is most likely to attract a reluctant
> viewer, because it literally transforms what, for some,
> might be a dry play into an expansive film and, at the
> same time, comments on the central difference between
> drama and film. In these opening images, Olivier
> acknowledges the original stage world of the drama and
> shows how the movies can transcend those dramatic limits.
> For viewers like myself, Shakespeare suddenly comes alive.

The useful rule of thumb here is to try to be aware of when and how your personal perspective and feelings enter your criticism and to what degree they are valuable or not, that is, when, those judgments seem to say something true not only for yourself but for others as well. A personal distaste for violence, say, or, for slow-paced stories could become a rich part of an essay when the writer carefully thinks through and offers reasons for that distaste. Or, my expectations, as someone who mainly sees slick Hollywood films, could be crucial in analyzing my slight confusion yet fascination with a film by the German filmmaker Rainer Werner Fassbinder, since other viewers often share that confusion.

In the examples used earlier, both Canby and Henderson openly introduce their own opinions and personalities into their arguments. Neither balks at using "I" to underline the presence of his perspective: "One may legitimately debate the validity of Mr. Malick's vision, but not, I think, his immense talent" (Canby); "I take an obvious point of departure: the film's voice-over narration by Holly. . . . This is, emphatically, just one approach to the film and not a privileged one" (Henderson). Canby's is perhaps a more opinionated "I", Henderson's more detached and cautious. Yet both Canby and Henderson use their personal positions to help form and energize their different responses to Malick's film. One might say that these uses of "I" are only the most forthright and direct indication of the many other evaluations and judgments that enter the essays: Canby's criticism of the romantic, junglelike setting where the two outlaws hide; Henderson's interest in narrative and theoretical questions about "performance."

When you write about the movies, personal feelings, expectations, and reactions can be the beginning of an intelligent critique, but they must be balanced with rigorous reflection on where those feelings and expectations and reactions come from and how they relate to more objective factors concerning the movie in question — its place in film history, its cultural background, its formal strategies. François Truffaut, both an intelligent filmmaker and a perceptive critic, has observed that "instead of indulging passions in criticism, one must at least try to be critical with some purpose. . . . What is interesting is not pronouncing a film good or bad, but explaining why."

Writing about film, then, is admittedly complex. It can also be exciting and rewarding. In 1908, Leo Tolstoy remarked about the movies: "You can see that this little clicking contraption with the revolving handle will make a revolution in our life — in the life of writers." Try to approach films with the same interest and shrewdness. Try to conceive of yourself as a writer with an equally purposeful and dynamic relationship with the movies you watch and enjoy.

2

Preparing to Watch and Preparing to Write

Of the several difficulties in writing about film, one of the most prominent is getting a handle on an experience that has so many layers. Put simply: What should you choose to analyze and to write about? the story? the acting? the editing? Watching a film can involve everything from the place where we see it and the price we pay to the size of the screen, the pace of the story, and the kind of music used as background for that story. In Jean Cocteau's words, "the cinema muse is too rich." As the first step toward an intelligent viewing, spectators need to break the habit of watching films "out of the corners of their eyes," as Cocteau puts it. This is where analysis begins.

Certainly our primary experience of a movie is the singular and perhaps private one of watching it for the first time — involved and enjoying it, one hopes, but possibly annoyed yet still somewhat involved. As the director in Godard's 1984 film *First Name: Carmen* (played by Godard himself) writes, "badly seen, badly said": seeing a movie with all your attention is the only way to begin writing about a film, even a film you don't like. Either as preparation before a screening or shortly afterward, a writer needs to sort out that personal and primary experience along manageable lines, and this sorting out should become the groundwork for an analysis of the movie. Should you talk about the characters? about technological innovations? about the film's effect on an audience? Where should you start to direct your attention and your analysis, so that you do not give yourself the impossible task of writing about the whole movie? Since the movies you see on the screen are a product of many forces — writers, production demands, the cost of technology, and hundreds of others — which in a sense precede the images you will be watching, it is necessary to approach those movies with sensitivity to some basic questions, influences, and problems. In the movies, much energy and time goes into "preproduction" activity, and your analysis will be better if you similarly spend at least some time on general preliminary questions. Prepare yourself for a movie; before it starts, ask about it and about your own potential interest in it.

1. As an art form, the movies involve literature, the pictorial and plastic arts, music, dance, theater, and even architecture. The student interested in architecture might thus respond keenly to an Eisenstein or Antonioni movie when he or she can direct that interest at how the filmmaker uses architectural space to add to the drama. A music or literature student might be drawn to certain art or experimental films or to the musical or literary features of a movie (Figure 1). Ask yourself which art forms most interest you and which you know the most about. Could you use your knowledge of literature or painting as a guide to a particular film? Might your interest in contemporary or classical music suggest that you look for a topic in movies like *True Stories* (1986), *Diva* (1982), *Amadeus* (1984), or *Truth or Dare* (1991)?

2. The film industry depends on and responds quickly to changes

Figure 1.   Visconti's *Death in Venice (1970)*, adapted from Thomas Mann's novella. What remains the same? What changes? How "literary" is the film?

in technology. Having grown used to contemporary Hollywood movies, most of us find that we react differently to a silent movie or a movie in black and white — an obvious example of how the early technology that produced these movies determines how we view them. Many other tools of the trade — sound technologies, color stocks, special effects — can likewise become the starting point for a revealing analysis. Whether a movie is made for a large screen or for a television screen can say a great deal about the story (note how epic movies like *The Ten Commandments* [1956] just don't seem the same on television). As some commentators have suggested, the technology behind *Star Wars* may be the most interesting aspect of that movie. If you are interested in technology, prepare to note features of the movie and its story that might depend on technology. Does the director make special use of black and white film stocks? Why? Does sound technology seem to play a large part in the movie? Is the movement (or lack of movement) of the camera related to the kind of camera used (as with the hand-held cameras of the French New Wave, which convey a sense of on-the-spot realism)? Usually these initial questions will require some later research and thinking to answer them adequately and to relate them to an analysis of the movie. But the student with some initial interest in the industrial and technological side of the movies will often find good material for a strong essay if he or she approaches movies on the lookout for the role technology plays in them.

3. Film technology, production, and distribution are commercial and economic enterprises. It is crucial to keep this in mind when approaching any movie. If, for instance, a viewer is going to see a low-budget, independent film (such as Michael Snow's *Wavelength* [1966-1967]) at the local art house, the expectations about that movie will and should be different from those about a glossy, $40-million epic (such as Michael Cimino's *Heaven's Gate* [1980]) at a showcase cinema. No film is necessarily good or bad because of its commercial or economic constraints and freedoms, but the ability to adjust one's expectations accordingly does allow a viewer to assess more accurately the achievements or failures of a movie. Thus, for third-world films from South America or Africa, the often

rough and unpolished look is not only an unavoidable by-product of financial constraints but, in some cases, it is also a conscious political sign used to distinguish these films from the glossy products of Hollywood. At the other end of the economic scale are the massive Hollywood productions whose gargantuan budgets mean that they must capture the largest possible audience, so these films take few risks that might alienate a part of that audience. Although this sort of angle on a movie will require some research if it is to be developed into essay material, an awareness of or sensitivity to the economic and commercial determinants behind any movie can prepare you for a more intelligent and complex response to the images on the screen. Be open-minded and suspicious: if it looks like a movie that was made inexpensively, does this reduced cost allow it to do and say things that a big-budget movie might not be able to? Conversely, how do some Hollywood movies take advantage of a big budget or make creative use of a small budget? Where is much of the money directed: the stars? the special effects? the promotion? and why? Does the film seem especially earthy or commercial, or does it try to reach a compromise between the two? Why? Who is the intended audience for the film: teenagers? the middle class? intellectuals? men? women?

Having these and other preliminary questions in mind when you sit down to watch a movie will sharpen and direct your analytical abilities. These questions can be a crucial guide through a first viewing, that difficult time when you are trying to determine what is worth writing about and what is not. On seeing D. W. Griffith's *The Birth of a Nation* (1915) for the first time, one student dismissed it as "a primitive and racist story with a lot of old-fashioned images"; another student simply accepted it as "almost a documentary about the Civil War and the Reconstruction." David Cook's analysis, however, is influenced by a sense of the historical complications and limitations of the movie, as well as by a sense of the presumption of a modern audience watching it many years later:

> In its monumental scale, in its concentration upon a crucial moment in American history, in its mixture of historical and invented characters, in its constant narrative movement between the epochal and the human, and, most significantly, in its chillingly accurate vision of an American

society predicated on race, *The Birth of a Nation* is a profoundly American epic. We can fault Griffith for badly distorting the historical facts of Reconstruction, for unconscionably stereotyping the American Negro as either fool or brute, and for glorifying a terrorist organization like the Klan, but we cannot quarrel with his basic assumption that American society was, and is, profoundly racist. That he endorses and encourages this situation rather than condemns it is properly repellent to contemporary audiences, as it was to many persons in 1915. But *we* must not allow our sympathies to obscure our own critical judgment, for then we make the same mistake as Griffith. And, as Americans, we must never overlook the possibility that the impetus for our most hostile reactions to Griffith's racism lies somewhere within our most deeply cherished illusions about ourselves. (79)

SUBJECT MATTER AND MEANING

These preliminary questions should remind you that the images you see are the product of certain influences and conditions and are not just the world seen through a frame. The movies are not just about a subject but about the rendition of that subject for particular reasons and to create certain meanings. Films are not just about a story, a character, a place, or a way of life; they are also what John Berger has called "a way of seeing" these elements in our lives. Any film at any point in history might describe a family, a war, or the conflict between races, but the ways these subjects are shown and the reasons they are shown in a particular way can vary greatly. These variations, through which a subject is given a specific meaning or meanings, are a large part of what analysis is concerned with. Why does the student who dismisses *The Birth of a Nation* later hail *The Deer Hunter* (1978), another film about a war involving races, as "one of the best movies ever made"? The subject is quite similar, but its meaning has changed significantly for that student.

To write an intelligent, perceptive analysis of the stories and characters in the movies, you must be prepared to see them as constructed according to certain forms and styles that arise from many historical influences. This is what analysis of the movies is fundamentally about: examining how a subject has been formed to mean something specific through the power of art, technology, and commerce. Be prepared to respond to those influences that most interest you. Be prepared with a questioning mind from the beginning.

SILENT DIALOGUE: TALKING BACK
TO THE MOVIES

Once the movie starts, your preliminary questions should become more and more specific regarding the movie you are watching and how it is constructed.

One of the most helpful techniques in preparing to write analytically about literature is the scribbling of marginal comments next to a text, the underlining we do, or simply the question marks we put next to difficult passages. No one approaches a book or a work of art with all the answers or even all the questions. Part of the excitement in viewing or reading a challenging work comes from the questions it provokes. Thomas De Quincey's "On the Knocking at the Gate in *Macbeth*" originates in a specific question that De Quincey asked himself after seeing a production of the play: "From my boyish days I had always felt a great perplexity on one point in *Macbeth*. It was this: The knocking at the gate which succeeds to the murder of Duncan produced to my feeling an effect for which I never could account." What, he asked himself, produced that effect? From that very specific question and a personal uncertainty comes one of the best essays ever written on Shakespeare.

This kind of questioning and annotating is one of the surest ways to begin an analysis of a movie. In contrast to literature, however, the special problem with film is that the images are constantly moving, so an analytic spectator must develop the habit of looking for key moments, patterns, or images within the film, even during a second or third viewing.

As you watch more films and grow more aware of differences and similarities, the right questions come more readily. At first, though, two guidelines may help initiate this dialogue with a movie:

- Note which elements of the movie strike you as unfamiliar or perplexing.
- Note which elements are repeated to emphasize a point or a perception.

Every movie uses patterns of repetition that are contrasted with striking singular moments. Recognizing these patterns and deciphering why they are important is a first step towards analyzing the meaning of a movie. Why, for instance, do so many scenes in *Rebel Without a Cause* (1956) take place in the family homes of the characters? Why, in *The Women* (1939), is black-and-white used for all the scenes except the fashion show? Even if you do not determine the answers to these questions while you are watching the movie, asking them is the key to a good analysis. These questions can be as elementary as:

- What does the title mean in relation to the story?
- Why does the movie start the way it does?
- When was the film made?
- Why are the opening credits presented in such a manner against this particular background?
- Why does the film conclude on this image?
- How is this movie similar to or different from the Hollywood movies I have seen recently or those of an older generation ?
- Does this film resemble any foreign films I know?
- Is there a pattern of striking camera movement, perhaps long shots or dissolves or abrupt transitions (see pp. 53–66)?
- Which three or four sequences are the most important?

When Andrew Sarris, a critic for the Village Voice, saw Martin Scorsese's *After Hours* (1985) he found the opening sequence not only bizarre but partly inexplicable; to some extent, his review evolves from that experience. Upon seeing Howard Hawks's *His Girl Friday* (1940) for the first time, most contemporary audiences would probably remark, and perhaps have difficulty with, the rapidity of the dialogue; following up this simple observation with careful thinking could bring some of the brilliance of this movie into focus. Terry Gilliam's *Brazil* (1985) is constructed through a series of strange images and questions about what is happening that viewers must deal with sooner or later if they are to make sense of the film: what is the relationship between the title and the story? what is the time frame of the story? can one distinguish between dreams and reality, and if not, why not? how would one describe the sets of this film? The number and nature of these questions — both about what you see and how it is shown — could vary infinitely depending on the movie or movies being discussed. Potentially, any and every aspect of a film is important. Talking about *You Only Live Once* (1937), Fritz Lang notes, for instance, a seemingly minor detail that, if the studio had allowed it to remain, would have focused upon a central theme in the film: "I wanted to have a kind of ironic touch when Fonda and Sidney flee from the law and she goes and buys him some cigarettes, which ultimately provide the means of his betrayal. I wanted her to buy Lucky Strike cigarettes to stress the irony of the bad luck they bring him." Learn to jot down information about props, costumes, camera positions, and so on, even during a first screening, and then choose the most telling evidence. These are the first steps in developing a strong and perceptive argument. Note how one student uses his questions about two striking features of *The Women* to focus a short analysis of that film:

Roger Malone

By most counts, The Women seems to be a standard movie about social relations in a 1930s society. There are, though, two odd twists to the movie that should catch anybody's eye: one, there is not a single man in the movie and, two, in the middle of this black-and-white film, there is a rather long fashion show sequence in full color. Why these twists, and are they something more than gimmicks?

The women at the heart of this movie are in some ways independent and resourceful. Their lives are not, though, "liberated" in any modern sense, for men are constantly being discussed and influencing the behavior of all the women. The physical absence of all the men from the screen consequently becomes an ironic way of suggesting how powerfully present those men are in the lives of women. For the women in this movie, even when men are not there, they are there.

The fashion show sequence seems related to this same idea. The sets, the costumes, and the actresses in The Women are all stunning, and the female characters

all seem concerned with how they and their surroundings appear — especially to men. What could be a more
accurate and appropriate centerpiece for the movie
than a fashion show of women showing other women how
to appear and what to wear? What could be a more
effective way to underline the importance of this
moment in the film than by making the only color
sequence in the movie?

The Women was made in 1939 by the same studio
that produced The Wizard of Oz the same year. In
The Women, however, the flight into color does not
last as long as Dorothy's, and for these women, the
yellow brick road is fashion itself. Through its
unusual twists, moreover, it seems to make a pretty
standard point: even when you cannot see behind the
curtain, at the center of the action, hiding there,
is still a man.

TAKING NOTES

Good film essays require more than one viewing, either of the film
itself or the usually more available videotape version (see pp. 130–131).
With one viewing, it is nearly impossible to see all the subtleties and
complexities in a movie and, at the same time, to take notes on this
information. Ideally, a first viewing should be a more or less note-free viewing
in which you enjoy the film on its most immediate level. With the second
screening, you can begin to take more careful and detailed notes.

Often, though, that needed second or third screening may not be
possible, especially when the film is older, foreign, or not in wide
distribution. In such cases, despite the difficulty in taking your eyes off the

screen momentarily, it is important to take notes of some sort during a first and only viewing. When more than one screening is possible, notes can be increasingly detailed and complete.

Preliminary notes can be simply a shorthand version of the questions and the dialogue a movie generates in your mind. No one can or wants to note everything that appears, especially when taking notes takes your eyes away from other information appearing on the screen. The trick is to learn to make economical use of your time and to recognize key sequences, shots, or narrative facts. (One useful exercise is to limit yourself to noting, with as much detail as possible, what you consider the three or four most important scenes, shots, or sequences in a film.) Depending on our interests, we will all respond to different points or figures in a movie (at least on one level), but most films offer recognizable dramatic moments or major themes that signal an audience to attend to what is happening: the opening sequence in *Citizen Kane* (1941) when "Rosebud" is first pronounced; the climactic death of the father in Sirk's *Written on the Wind* (1957); the use of sound in Lang's *M* (1931); the dramatic impact of isolated scenes between Bogart and Bacall in practically any of their movies; or the explosive moment when Mookie breaks the window of the pizza parlor in Spike Lee's *Do the Right Thing* (1989). Even when a film denies or parodies dramatic moments or themes — as in Chantal Akerman's *Jeanne Dielmann* (1977) or in many Antonioni films — those variations from the norm can become the central point that a viewer should attempt to make sense of.

In noting this kind of information, be as specific and concrete as possible. Record not only the figures and objects in the frame (the content), but how the frame itself and its photographic qualities (the form) are used to define that content through camera angles, lighting, the use of depth and surface, and editing techniques. A person preparing to write about *Meet Me in St. Louis* (1944) might note the father's role in this family of women or the odd, macabre scenes with the youngest daughter, Tootie. With practice, however, that writer would also be able to jot down information about the theatrical use of space in specific scenes or the spectacular use of bright color. Similarly, a student new to R. W. Fassbinder's films would probably catch some of the major motifs or salient moments in the story of *The Marriage of Maria Braun* (1979): the numerous ironic turns in sexual relations that seem so bound up with financial matters or the confusion about whether, at the conclusion, the heroine does or does not commit suicide. A bit more advanced viewer, however, might also remark on the careful overlapping and disjunctions between the sound track and the images: perhaps the student will describe the subtle but powerful scene in which Oswald casually plays a concerto measure on a piano that alternates with the same phrase in the sound track's background music, or perhaps he or she will note how, during that melodramatic closing sequence, the radio in the background blares a World Cup championship match.

Most writers develop a shorthand system for technical information: "p.o.v. " for *point of view shot* and "l.s." for *long shot* (a shot that shows, for example, the whole of a figure from a distance, as opposed to a close-up of a face or a hand). These are easy to learn and use when taking notes (the abbreviations do not, of course, appear in your essay):

cu	close-up (showing only a character's head, for example)
xcu	extreme close-up (showing perhaps a detail of that head, such as the eyes)
ms	medium shot (somewhere between a close-up and a full shot, showing most but not all of a figure)
fs	full or long shot (revealing a character's entire body in the frame)
3/4s	three-quarter shot (showing only about three-quarters of the characters' bodies)
ps	pan shot (the point of view pivots from left to right, or vice versa, without changing its vertical axis)
s/rs	shot/reverse shot pattern (the point of view shows, for example, a person looking at someone and then shows the individual being looked at)
ct	cut (when the film changes from one image to another)
lt	long take (the film does not cut to another image for an unusually long time)
trs	tracking shot (the entire point of view moves, on tracks or a dolly, following, for instance, a walking figure); you can indicate the direction that the camera tracks by using arrows:

crs   crane shot (the point of view of an outdoor scene filmed from high above)

la   low angle (the point of view is low, tilted upward)

ha   high angle (the point of view is above, tilted downward); the exact angle can be made clearer by using arrows

Ultimately, each individual develops a personal shorthand and other abbreviations to record accurately the details of a scene or sequence (these and other terms are defined in Chapter 3). Often, for annotations on sound or dialogue, a key phrase or word may be what allows you to make a more precise description of the scene or sequence later. Sometimes these annotations may even take the form of a sketch, as with this student's attempt to note how, in this sequence of five shots (Figures 2–6) from *Potemkin* (1925), Eisenstein's editing of the soldiers' attack on a mother and child works to create conflicts in the movement in each shot:

Figure 2.   cu—sold. legs

Figure 3.   fs—sold/moth. & ch.

Figure 4.   ms—moth. & ch.

Figure 5   fs—sold./moth. & ch.

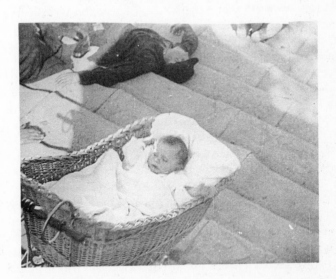

Figure 6.   ms—baby

No one will want to annotate an entire film. Anticipating a specific argument and essay, everyone will focus on relevant kinds of information, from themes and characters to technical elements and editing structures. A writer who wishes to analyze the famous shower sequence in Hitchcock's *Psycho* (1960), for instance, might make preliminary notes that look something like this: (1) m.s. Marion and Norman, cramped space, "trapped," birds, eyes, sexual tension; (2) classical painting/peep hole; (3) 90° c.u. then p.o.v. N. at undressing M.; (4) shower, tight space; (5) murder: quick cuts, c.u.'s knife, face, flesh, M's p.o.v.; (6) M. clawing curtain, c.u. drain, c.u. eye. This is a sketch that needs to be filled in later. If a second viewing is possible, more dialogue or details could be added. Yet, beginning with these notes, a writer could develop a fairly sophisticated and rigorous reading of this key scene.

VISUAL MEMORY AND REFLECTION

Preliminary notes and sketches will form the basis for a good argument, however, only if the writer elaborates on them soon after seeing the movie by filling in the shorthand with more measured descriptions. Jean Mitry, the renowned French film historian, once said his most important asset was an unusually precise visual memory. The best writers about film either come equipped with or learn to develop a sharp auditory and visual memory, one which allows them to recall details about a movie. (Remember: a memory can be trained and developed; no one should justify careless viewing and annotation by claiming a "bad memory.") The sooner one can go back to those preliminary notes, the better, for then the memory can be triggered to add specifics and place images in the context of the larger story and other narrative issues. Returning to the *Psycho* notes, the writer might recall other images that emphasize eyes in the movie and thus make connections between the hole in the wall and the close-up of the shower drain or between the cramped space of Norman's den and that of the shower. He or she might realize that the sequence is remarkably balanced and frighteningly logical in being extended as it is until the final close-ups of the dark drain and the dead Marion's open eye. Upon further reflection, the writer might decide that, based on the opening shots of the film, *Psycho* is about "looking" and the sexual or gendered implications of looking.

When you've reviewed your notes, the shape and direction of your argument could begin to appear: an idea of what you wish to say about the movie. Whether or not you were prepared before a first viewing, possible arguments and topics should present themselves as you add to and develop your preliminary notes. In reviewing notes on a film by Ozu, a Japanese director, for instance, you may remark (possibly with discomfort) on the slow pacing of the film, its concerns with family structure, or the low camera placement — any and all of which observations could, after some thinking, become a starting point for a complex essay about Ozu's distinctive themes and style. While going over notes on *The Marriage of Maria Braun,* one student discovered that her initial perception of the movie as a glossy melodrama was complicated by those strange technical maneuvers with the sound track that she recorded in her notes; her essay then discussed the ways in which the sound track signaled the splits and divisions between the main character's private, emotional life and her public, social life (Figure 7). Finally, the writer on *Psycho* begins to focus an essay on looking and sexuality with the central shower sequence: *Psycho* becomes a film about the violence implicit in the sexual and gendered dynamics of men and women looking at each other, and Marion's murder becomes the most dramatic example of people trapped in the violence and horror of their sexuality. Consider how Donald Spoto refined his notes:

Figure 7. *The Marriage of Maria Braun*: A melodrama made cramped and uncomfortable by the camera framing.

The psychological shock of the sequence, however, derives from the fact that the character with whom we have identified has been brutally eliminated. We have felt her frustration, hoped she would escape the police, enjoyed her innocent teasing of Norman, shared her sense of release at the decision to make amends and experienced the first moments of that cleansing shower. And, through Hitchcock's brilliant direction, we have felt her hideous pain, and her inability to avoid the persistent stabs as she turns around in the shower. The cleansing water turns to blood. We have followed every step of the way in her descent from the banal to the horrific. Now, seeing her last sight through her eyes, we watch her left hand slowly sliding down the tiles in a last attempt to "scratch and claw," as Norman has put it, out of this shower-turned-coffin. She slowly turns and, leaning against the wall with her last breaths, slides down into death. She stares, with gradually closing lids, than reaches out — for us. But we pull back, so she grabs the shower curtain for final support, ripping it from the hooks as she falls forward and over the edge of the tub. One more glance at the cleansing laver, from a point under the shower nozzle, and then — in one of the most brilliant images in any film — we follow the bloodied water spiralling down the drain. In an extraordinary lap dissolve, we emerge from the darkness of the drain out from behind her eye, open and stilled in death. The journey into the depths of the "normal" psyche has ended in tragedy. The veneer of normality has been shattered at her (and our) peril. And the close-up of the eye links us by association with Norman's eye during the peeping scene earlier, and with our own role throughout as peeping Toms. All the characters of this film are indeed one character, and through the use of alternating subjective camera technique, that character is the individual viewer. (372-374)

Few of us are inclined to work back through our notes immediately after seeing a movie. Yet a prompt review of one's notes is extremely useful and could make the difference between a dull and hazy response to a film and a compelling and subtle one. Methodical notes allow a viewer to map accurately what happens in a movie, to record details about the subject and its meaning that would otherwise soon fade from memory. Unless one has continual access to the film or a script, it is difficult to retain these facts, and, without them, anything you have to say will probably appear much too impressionistic. When you go over the film and the key sequences in your notes, ideas begin to take shape. When you can support those ideas with concrete descriptions from the movie, your argument becomes dramatically more convincing.

3

Film Terms and Topics

Developing a sense of how to question movie images and take notes on them goes hand in hand with an ability to direct those questions toward specific topics for analysis. Questions and notes should lead to more questions and to partial or full answers. This path leads to an essay focused on particular themes and techniques in a movie. A major part of this process is developing a vocabulary with which to ask your questions properly, a terminology to describe what you see and think, words to help you focus and organize your analysis. Being able to notice and then comment on an instance of "crosscutting" in *Silence of the Lambs* (1991) or to describe the "narrative structure" in the Taviani brothers' *Padre Padrone* (1977) is not just good for classroom conversation; it allows a writer to make finer, more accurate discriminations and evaluations and to situate a film within the larger tradition of film history and analysis. These kinds of discriminations should point you towards an essay topic.

Every discipline has its own special language or use of words, which allows it to discuss its subject with precision and subtlety. A literary critic, for example, needs to distinguish between a metaphor and a simile, since each term describes a different rhetorical figure that, in turn, refers to different perceptions: to write "My love is like a red, red rose" (simile) is different from "My love is a red, red rose" (metaphor), and the person who can appreciate that difference will read and interpret those lines better. Similarly, a knowledgeable basketball fan will be able to summarize quickly and evaluate the action of a game if he or she knows a specialized vocabulary that includes terms like "jump shot," "pick," and "fast break."

With film, too, a critical vocabulary allows you to view a movie more accurately and to formulate your perceptions more easily. Consider the term "frame." In writing about film, *frame* refers to the rectangle that contains the image: the frame of the movie screen itself, which does not change during a movie, and, more important, the camera frame, which regularly changes its relationship to the objects being filmed. Being aware of this term and its uses, you will be more sensitive to how the camera frame controls what you see and how you see it. You will be able to note how the camera frame may include certain actions and exclude others, how the angle at which it is placed or its distance from a person can add considerably to what the filmmaker is trying to say. One student observed this of a recent movie: "Although the scene seems to be a typical family gathering, the viewer becomes aware that something is wrong or un-settled because the camera frame is slightly off balance and unusually crowded with characters and furniture." What may sometimes go unnoticed is brought to light through the accurate use of a term.

Themes

Going over your notes, you may wish first to identify the *themes* of the movie, which often comes down to stepping back and asking what this film is "about": the triumph of good over evil in *Star Wars* (1977), for example, or the tragic confusions of war in *Platoon* (1986). Themes, in many cases, become the foundation for an analysis, because they point to the main ideas that inform a movie. They are not, strictly speaking, the "moral" or message of the movie; they are the large and the small ideas that help explain the actions and events in it. Ask, for example:

- Who are the central characters?
- What do they represent in themselves and in relation to each other? the importance of individuality or society? human strength or human compassion?
- How do the characters' actions create a story with meaning or a constellation of meanings?
- Does the story emphasize the benefits of change or endurance?
- What kind of life or what actions does the film ask you to value or criticize, and why?
- If there is no coherent message or story, why not?
- How does the movie make you feel? happy? depressed? confused? and why?

Having stated a principal theme in a film (and perhaps one or two subsidiary themes), a writer needs to explain them in terms of the specific situation and aims of the movie. The more sensitive a writer's vocabulary, the more refined the perception and argument will be. Thus, "alienation" may very well describe the broadest thematic lines of Chaplin's *City Lights* (1931), Capra's *You Can't Take It with* You (1938), Woody Allen's *Shadows and Fog* (1992), and Bertolucci's *The Conformist* (1970). Although this may be a good start, however, a sharp analysis demands that the writer make finer distinctions about the historical, stylistic, and structural ways that theme is manifested in each movie. Does that alienation seem inevitable, perhaps even desirable? Does it lead to new knowledge or is it a disaster that could have been avoided? Is it presented as a tragic or comic problem in the movie? Writing about *The Conformist,* a student might develop the theme of alienation by observing that here it relates to the protagonist's sexuality and the fascist period in Italy and that, unlike the first two movies (and to some extent in the third), the movie never really resolves this alienation. The writer might extend that argument by describing how the main character regularly seems entrapped and isolated by the rigorous framing of the camera (Figure 8), and by the many frames

Figure 8. The frames within the framing of *The Conformist*.

within the image as a whole (door frames, window frames, etc.). Note, however, that this kind of consideration of alienation in *The Conformist* does not attempt to fashion a simplified and inappropriate moral. One cannot conclude that "in *The Conformist,* alienation is an evil which dooms the character to misery."

While identifying themes provides an important foundation for your analysis, writing about the movies involves a wide range of special terms that will help you organize and clarify your topic. The remainder of this chapter will discuss the most important of these terms as they are used to discuss four dimensions of the movies:

1. The connections between the movies and other artistic traditions, such as literature and painting
2. The theatrical dimension of the film image, or its mise-*en*-scène
3. The composition of the movie achieved through camera positions and editing
4. The use of sound in the film

Depending on your topic, any or all of these dimensions and their vocabulary could be central to your essay.

FILM AND THE OTHER ARTS

Although the movies are one of the youngest of the arts, they have absorbed the structures and forms of many older arts. Not surprisingly, therefore, writing about film requires some of the critical language of these other literary and visual arts: we speak of "plot" and "character" in both films and novels, and terms such as "point of view" are part of the critical vocabulary of painting, literature, and the movies. Borrowed terminology allows a critic to make important connections with other fields, but it also demands that a writer be sensitive to how terms and structures change when they are applied to film. Here we will look at three related terms that film studies share with the literary and visual arts: *narrative, character,* and *point of view.*

Narrative

When most of us refer to the movies, we often have in mind narrative movies, not documentaries or experimental films. A *narrative* has two principal components:

- The *story* is all the events that are presented to us or that we can infer have happened.
- The *plot* is the arrangement or construction of those events in a certain order or structure.

All films that sketch the life of Napoleon would tell the same story, describing his birth, his rise to power, the French Revolution, its aftermath, and his exile to Elba. The plots in these different movies could, however, be structured and arranged in various ways: one might begin with Napoleon's last days at Elba and tell his story through a series of flashbacks, showing events that occurred earlier than ones already shown; another might start with his birth and move chronologically through his life.

Always ask yourself how the narrative of the film you are watching is constructed. Is it a movie with a story line? If not, why not? Is the story told chronologically, or does the plot rearrange events in an unusual temporal order? Is there a reason for the particular plot structure? What in the story is left out in the actual plot construction? Are there reasons for including some material and omitting other material? Does the way in which the story is told become a prominent feature of the film and thus a central factor in an analysis of it? How do you recognize the narrative structure: is there a voice-over in which a character's voice describes events, thereby making it clear that he or she is organizing the plot? Are there technical elements that give dramatic indications about the way the story is structured, such as the change from black and white to color in *The Wizard of Oz* or Abel Gance's use of three screens in his *Napoleon?* What propels the story: a mystery as in *The Big Sleep* (1946)? a desire to reach a goal, as in *The Wizard of Oz?* Is it difficult to determine this, as in some modern movies in which the plot seems to have no definite direction?

The various relationships between a story, its plot, and a narrative style are numerous. When most of us think of a narrative film, however, we probably have in mind what is often called the classical narrative. To discuss any kind of film narrative it is useful to have some sense of this important narrative form. A classical narrative usually has:

1. A plot development in which there is a logical relationship between one event and another
2. A sense of closure at the end (a happy or a tragic ending, for example)
3. Stories that are focused on characters
4. A narrative style that attempts to be more or less objective

Not all classical narratives are the same, of course, and many fine essays are about the variations and innovations within this model. For instance, they may discuss the role of class in these stories or the ambiguous endings in others. One student began his paper on Howard Hawks's *The Big Sleep* by observing:

                                                            Bill Evans

    This classic mystery story does not make complete
sense. It seems as if the complicated plot has lost
track of the story, and frequently it is very difficult to follow the logic of who killed whom and why.
Nonetheless, The Big Sleep remains a model of classical filmmaking in the way it concentrates all the
action on the main characters, Bogart and Bacall. If
the plot is confused, these characters make you
forget that confusion and realize that the story is
about them.

In the following paragraphs, Gerald Mast looks at narrative structure as it applies to many Hawks films, such as *To Have and Have Not* (1944) and *His Girl Friday*. Note how Mast first places his analysis in the literary tradition of narrative, then moves to a discussion of plots constructed upon the notion of "surprising inevitability."

> What is a good story? First, there is the construction of an action — not just enumerating a string of events but organizing those events into a coherent and powerful shape. The construction of a narrative action relies on a very interesting paradox, of which Hawks was well aware. On the one hand, the events in a narrative must seem to flow spontaneously, naturally, surprisingly; nothing must be expected, nothing foreseen. On the other hand, the events in a narrative must be prepared for, motivated, foreshadowed; nothing is unexpected, everything foreseen. On the one hand, everything that happens to King Lear is a surprise; On the other, everything in the play proceeds from Kent's command in the beginning

to "See better, Lear." It is surprising that Emma Woodhouse discovers that it is Mr. Knightley whom she really must marry; yet everything in *Emma* points the way to this inevitable and inescapable discovery. The paradox of narrative construction is that it synthesizes the accidents of nature — which seem random — and the patterns of logic — which are fixed; the outcome of events is simultaneously inevitable yet surprising to the reader or viewer when the inevitable occurs. The narrative that is insufficiently spontaneous and surprising is familiarly condemned as contrived, overplotted, unnatural, and stilted; the narrative that is insufficiently patterned is familiarly condemned as random, wandering, arbitrary, and formless.

How does Hawks's story construction relate to this paradox of surprising inevitability? In over forty years of filmmaking, collaborating with over a dozen major writers, Howard Hawks builds every story in an identical four-part structure. The first part is a prologue that either (1) establishes the conflict in a past or present close relationship of the major characters (this is the usual pattern of Ben Hecht's scripts for Hawks) or (2) initiates a conflict by the collision of two apparently opposite characters upon their initial meeting (this is the usual Furthman-Faulkner pattern). The second and third parts develop the central conflict established in the first, either by letting one of the conflicting characters or life styles dominate in the second part, then the other in the third, or by letting one of the characters work alone in the second part, then both of them together in the third. And the fourth section resolves the central conflict, often by a return to the original physical setting of the prologue, but in which setting the warring characters now see themselves and one another in a new light. Occasionally Hawks adds a very brief epilogue or "tag" to return the narrative full circle to its beginning. Whatever else one can say about this narrative structure, it gives a Hawks story the firmness of shape, the elegance, economy, and symmetry that allow surprising events to transpire within the firm logic and structure of a controlled pattern. (30–31)

Not all movies are classical narratives or even narratives; some movies are *nonnarrative*, meaning they do not tell stories. Experimental films, for example, may avoid stories and investigate questions unrelated to narrative, such as the abstract patterns of light and shadow on film. Documentary films that may present real events, such as a typical day at a factory or the religious ritual of an Indian tribe, without organizing those events as a story. In addition, many movies create narratives that are outside the classical tradition or that may intentionally confront that tradition in order to tell their stories in a distinctive manner.

When you watch a movie that seems to avoid a traditional story line or that appears to tell its story in an unusual or perhaps confusing way, ask yourself how the movie is organizing its plot and narration and what it is trying to achieve. Does the story seem illogical, as in some Buñuel films in which events follow the logic of a dream? Does the narrative seem to be telling two or more stories that are difficult to connect, such as in *Hiroshima Mon Amour* (1959), in which the story of a woman and her Nazi lover is told alongside the story of the bombing of Hiroshima? Does the movie have a confusing beginning or an unresolved conclusion? Why? How do these or other narrative strategies relate to the stories being told? With *Hiroshima Mon Amour*, a writer might, after some thought, begin by observing that both stories concern World War II and are told by two newly met lovers; the difficulty in the narrative structure might then be related to the woman's pain in organizing and communicating her memories to someone who comes from a different culture but with a similar historical crisis. Once you have learned to recognize classical narrative forms, you should be more aware of how stories can be told in a variety of other ways.

Characters

Characters are a common topic for analysis in literature, drama, and film. They are the individuals who populate narrative and nonnarrative films. Whether they are main characters or minor characters, they normally focus the action and often the themes of a movie (Figure 9). Often a discussion of film concentrates on what happens to the characters or how they change. In a movie like *My Dinner with André* (1981), which films the dinner conversation between two men, the movie could more accurately be described as being about two characters telling stories rather than a story about two characters. Keep in mind that an analysis of characters in a movie can be boring or seem simpleminded when you approach them as though they are merely reflections of real people or when you blur the difference between the star and the character. Yet, if you remain attuned to the variety in character types, you will begin to see subtleties and complications in how characters function and what they can mean in different films. As an exercise, consider the characters portrayed by Lillian Gish in *Broken Blossoms* (1919), Lauren Bacall in *The Big Sleep,* and Diane Keaton in *Annie Hall* (1977) and describe how and why those characters are so different.

Figure 9.   *Fellini's Casanova* is primarily about the lavish masquerades and passions of one character.

You can begin an analysis of characters by asking yourself whether those characters seem or are meant to seem realistic. What makes them realistic? Are they defined by their clothes, their conversation, or something else? If they do not appear to be realistic, why not, and why are they meant to seem strange or fantastic? Do the characters fit the setting of the story? Does the movie focus on one or two characters, as in *The Big Sleep,* or on many, as in *Nashville,* in which there doesn't seem to be a central character? Do the characters change? in what ways? What values do the characters seem to represent, that is, what do they say about such matters as independence, sexuality, and political belief? These are the kinds of questions you will want to consider in order to make more sense of characters and determine why they are important.

Point of View

Like narrative, *point of view* is a term that film shares with the literary and visual arts. In the broadest sense it refers to the position from which something is seen and, by implication, how that point of view determines what you see. In the simplest sense, the point of view is purely physical. My point of view regarding a house across the street will be very different when I look from the rooftop of my house than when I look from the basement window. In a more sophisticated sense, point of view can be psychological or cultural: a child's point of view regarding a dentist's office will probably not be the same as an adult's.

In the same way, we can talk about the point of view that a camera has in relationship to a person or an action and even the point of view that a narrative directs at its subject. Movies commonly use an *objective point of view,* whereby most of what is shown is not confined to any one person's perspective. In *Gone with the Wind* (1939) and *Lawrence of Arabia* (1962), the audience sees scenes and events (the battle of Atlanta, Lawrence's journeys) that are supposedly objective in their scope and accuracy, beyond the knowledge or perspective of any one person. In specific scenes, however, that audience may be aware that they are seeing another character only through Rhett's or Lawrence's eyes, and at these times, the camera is recreating that individual's *subjective point of view*. Some movies might experiment with the possibilities of point of view: in *Apocalypse Now* (1979), we seem to see the entire story from Captain Willard's (Martin Sheen's) point of view; he introduces the story as something that has already happened to him, but despite this indication of historical objectivity many of the scenes recreate his very personal, nightmarish perspective on the war in Vietnam (Figure 10).

Point of view is central to writing about films because films are basically about seeing the world in a certain way. Approach point of view by using two general guidelines:

1. Notice how and when the camera creates the point of view of an individual character.
2. Notice whether the story is told mostly from an objective point of view or from the subjective perspective of one single person.

Ask yourself in what ways the point of view determines what you see. Does it limit or prejudice your vision in any way? What can you tell about the characters through whose eyes you see? Are they aggressive? suspicious? clever? in love?

Figure 10.   A narrative structured on the point of view of the central character, Captain Willard *(Apocalypse Now)*.

Because the movies incorporate the traditions of books, plays, and even sculpture and painting, such concepts as narrative, character, and point of view are not only useful but necessary in analyzing film. Often they are the basis for a comparative essay that examines a movie and its adaptation as a film. Other essays might compare different film versions of one story or a group of films by one director. When you write a comparative essay of this kind, be sensitive to and careful about not only how these terms connect art forms, but how they highlight differences. Be aware of how the film medium might change the message of an original book or play: look at how a literary or artistic achievement is translated successfully into a movie, and consider what may have been lost. To compare the film *Apocalypse Now* and the short novel *Heart of Darkness* (1898), a writer may choose to discuss the subjective point of view that describes one Captain Willard's journey through Vietnam and the other Captain Willard's — Marlowe's — journey into Africa. That comparison will be much sharper and more revealing if the writer can show how certain literary techniques (long sentences full of repetitions, for example) create one point of view and how certain film techniques (the use of light and shadow, for instance) create the other. These film techniques are the subject of the rest of this chapter.

MISE-EN-SCÈNE AND REALISM

The *mise-en-scène,* a French term roughly translated as "what is put into the scene" (put before the camera), refers to all those properties of a cinematic image that exist independently of camera position, camera movement, and editing (although a viewer will see these dimensions united in one image). Mise-en-scène includes lighting, costumes, sets, the quality of the acting, and other shapes, objects, and characters in the scene. Many writers mistakenly believe that these theatrical features are a somewhat unsophisticated topic for analysis, because they appear to be more a part of a dramatic tradition than a part of a cinematic tradition. For some writers, evaluating the performance of an actor can seem much less important than analyzing the narrative or the camera work. For other critics, the tools and terms of mise-en-scène are the keys to the important features of any movie.

Realism

The major reason for our tendency to overlook or to undervalue mise-en-scène in the movies is the powerful illusion of realism that is at the heart of the film medium. We often presume that "what is put into the scene" is simply what is there, and we conclude that it cannot be analyzed in the way we would analyze the construction of a plot. We accept the New York setting of *An Unmarried Woman* (1977) as a natural background, the apartment where the main characters live as their natural residence. The illusion of realism, in short, is a kind of mise-en-scène that makes us believe that the images are of an everyday world that is simply "there" — one we know and are familiar with. Allardyce Nicoll has described the problem:

> In the cinema we demand something different. Probably we carry into the picture-house prejudices deeply ingrained in our beings. The statement that "the camera cannot lie" has been disproved by millions of flattering portraits and by dozens of spiritualistic pictures which purport to depict fairies but which mostly turn out to be faintly disguised pictures of ballet-dancers or replicas of figures in advertisements of night-lights. Yet in our

heart of hearts we credit the truth of that statement. A picture, a piece of sculpture, a stage-play — these we know were created by man; we have watched the scenery being carried in back stage and we know we shall see the actors, turned into themselves again, bowing at the conclusion of the performance. In every way the "falsity" of a theatrical production is borne in upon us, so that we are prepared to demand nothing save a theatrical truth. For the films, however, our orientation is vastly different. Several periodicals, it is true, have endeavored to let us into the secrets of the moving-picture industry and a few favored spectators have been permitted to make the rounds of the studios; but from ninety per cent of the audience the actual methods employed in the preparation of a film remain far off and dimly realised. . . .

The strange paradox, then, results: that, although the cinema introduces improbabilities and things beyond nature at which any theatrical director would blanch and murmur soft nothings to the air, the filmic material is treated by the audience with far greater respect (in its relation to life) than the material of the stage. Our conceptions of life in Chicago gangsterdom and in distant China are all colored by films we have seen. What we have witnessed on the screen becomes the "real" for us. In moments of sanity, maybe, we confess that of course we do not believe this or that, but, under the spell again, we credit the truth of these pictures even as, for all our professed superiority, we credit the truth of newspaper paragraphs. . . . (35-38)

You must learn, however, to suspect realism in the movies, since it can distract you from the many interesting possibilities that mise-en-scène analysis offers. Watching a documentary from a foreign country or an old movie once considered realistic, you recognize how relative your sense of realism is and how — even when the filmmaker might not acknowledge it — the reality of a movie is constructed for a purpose. Simply putting a camera in front of a scene, as one writer has noted, changes the most realistic situation into a theatrical setting. Asked to look more closely at the realism of *An Unmarried Woman,* one student thus corrected her original perception and observed how the mise-en-scène of New York City was not just where these characters lived:

Anna M. Lee

The setting of New York City is, in fact, divided
into two parts reflecting the different instincts of
the female lead: the fashionable, upper-middle-class

world of the Upper East Side and the artsy, bohemian
climate of Soho and Greenwich Village. The various
apartments she enters or lives in reflect a similar
division: the opulent and well furnished home, with its
bright, picture-window views, and the darker, funkier
rooms of her artist friends. Eventually, it seems, she
finds a perfect compromise in the right lover and the
right apartment: clean, brightly lit, and spacious;
full of paintings and the counter-cultural charm of
futons and pillow furniture.

Whether the movie is a documentary or a realistic Hollywood film, a practiced eye might begin an analysis by asking basic questions about the theatrics of realism and how it is used (Figure 11). Why does the movie try to seem realistic? How does it try to create a realistic scene? What is

Figure 11. *Gimmie Shelter* (1977) is a documentary that focuses on the thin line between theatrics and realism — and the sometimes dangerous relationship between the two.

included, and what is left out? What realistic details in the mise-en-scène — the clothing, the homes, the props, the outdoor world — relate to the actions of the characters or the themes of the movie? Treat the mise-en-scène of realistic films with the same analytical sense you might direct at a stage play, where costumes and sets are never selected casually

Elements of Mise-en-Scène

In any film, from the most realistic to the most theatrical, there will be specific properties of the mise-en- scène to which you can direct your attention and from which good essay topics will come.

Settings and *sets* denote the location or the construction of a location where a scene is filmed. With some movies, you will notice immediately the importance of the setting and the sets. In *The Cabinet of Dr. Caligari* (1919), the expressionist set design may be far more interesting for some viewers than the characters or the structure of the story: the sets are obviously painted buildings and streets whose distorted angles and shapes are meant to suggest the mental imbalance and social chaos of the characters. One might make the same case for a movie like *Alien* (1979), in which the elaborately twisted passageways of the spaceship and the mysterious construction where the characters discover the alien eggs reverberate with a symbolic significance associated with women and mother-hood. In a more ironic manner, Hitchcock uses his settings as commentaries on the plot and characters. In the climactic moments of *North by Northwest* (1959), the hero and heroine climb across the gigantic faces of the presidents on Mt. Rushmore; in a movie about U.S. security and government, this setting is not only spectacular but central to the themes of the movie. In these ways, settings can be much more than background, and a writer interested in the use of sets and settings should start with two questions:

- Do the objects and props in the setting, whether natural (like rivers and trees) or artificial (like paintings and buildings), have a special significance that relates to the characters or the story?
- Does the arrangement of objects, props, and characters within that setting have some significance? (for example, are they crowded together? do inanimate objects seem to have a life, as they might in a Chaplin movie?)

Although most good films will give the setting and its objects nearly as much meaning as the characters, films differ greatly in how they use their settings in relation to the characters and the stories. Sets and settings may suggest historical realism, as in *Louisiana Story* (1948) (Figure 12), or provide images of a character's mind, as in *The Cabinet of Dr. Caligari*, or become more complex and important than the story or the characters, as perhaps in *Batman* (1989). In writing about setting, however, one must do more than describe it: one must seek to discover its significance in relation to the themes of the film or to other aspects of the film (its production, the intended audience). Such a focus will help to explain why the setting and the way it is constructed are important.

Use the same rule of thumb in discussing other elements of the mise-en-scène: whether your interest is acting styles, costumes, or lighting, precise descriptions must be coupled with a sense of why they are important and how they add to the meaning of the movie, that is, how they can become a significant topic for analysis. We all know that an actor is the individual who plays the part of a character in the movie. But *acting style* — how an actor plays a part — will differ considerably from film to film and from one decade to the next. Looked at thoughtfully, acting style can be a challenging topic to address or a target for focusing an analysis of

Figure 12.   In *Louisiana Story*, the sets and the setting evoke a kind of historical realism.

a specific movie. A writer might, for instance, compare the acting style in an Italian neorealist movie such as *Open City* (1945), in which the actors are often people chosen precisely because they have no acting experience, with the very mannered style of a British or American actor, such as Meryl Streep, whose notion of a realistic performance includes a great deal of studied artifice. Carl Dreyer said, "There is no greater experience in a studio than to witness the expression of a sensitive face under the mysterious power of inspiration"; in the following paragraphs, Roland Barthes describes the acting style expressed in the face of Greta Garbo:

> Garbo still belongs to that moment in cinema when capturing the human face still plunged audiences into the deepest ecstasy, when one literally lost oneself in a human image as one would in a philtre, when the face represented a kind of absolute state of the flesh, which could be neither reached nor renounced. A few years earlier the face of Valentino was causing suicides; that of Garbo still partakes of the same rule of Courtly Love, where the flesh gives rise to mystical feelings of perdition.
>
> It is indeed an admirable face-object. In *Queen Christina,* a film which has again been shown in Paris in the last few years, the make-up has the snowy thickness of a mask: it is not a painted face, but one set in plaster, protected by the surface of the colour, not by its lineaments. Amid all this snow at once fragile and compact, the eyes alone, black like strange soft flesh, but not in the least expressive, are two faintly tremulous wounds. In spite of its extreme beauty, this face, not drawn but sculpted in something smooth and friable, that is, at once perfect and ephemeral, comes to resemble the flour-white complexion of Charlie Chaplin, the dark vegetation of his eyes, his totem-like countenance. (56)

Costumes, or the clothes the characters wear, can vary along a spectrum from realistic dress to extravagant fantasy; often they provide a writer with a key to a character's identity. James Bond may often wear a tuxedo, and Sylvester Stallone's Rocky prefers to wear as little as possible; in both cases, we learn something about the character from the costume — that one is socially sophisticated and the other is instinctual. Some films, like The *Rocky Horror Picture Show* (1976) and *Tootsie* (1982), are largely about costuming and changing appearances through dress and make-up, and both films are about how men dress like women to confront or deal with conventional attitudes about sexual roles. White hats no longer necessarily indicate a good character, but you should continue to question why characters look and dress the way they do. Do their costumes suggest how they view themselves or how they wish to be viewed by others? Does a character change clothing, as in *Saturday Night Fever* (1977), when John Travolta becomes a different person by donning his dancing clothes at night? Do those changes tell you anything about the personality or the society? Is there a special feature of a costume, such as the baseball glove that identifies Steve McQueen in *The Great Escape* (1963), which helps you to analyze that character? Do not take the costume element of the mise-en-scène for granted.

Lighting comprises the various ways in which a character or an object or a scene can be illuminated, either by natural sunlight or by artificial sources such as lamps. It allows a filmmaker to direct a viewer's attention in a certain way or to create a certain atmosphere. We all recognize such distinctions as the difference between the bright lighting of an outdoor scene in a western and the shadowy darkness of the alleyways of a gangster film. We probably notice how in the first case the lighting creates a feeling of clarity and optimism and in the second a feeling of oppression and gloom. A more demanding task would be to note and analyze the more subtle gradations and patterns of film lighting that do not dramatically call attention to themselves. In Betrand Tavernier's *Sunday in the Country* (1985), the softly lit interiors and exteriors are meant to recreate the lighting found in Impressionist paintings, a vision of the world that the painter-grandfather of that movie knows is fading. In Stanley Kubrick's *Barry Lyndon* (1978), some scenes use very low light (candlelight, in fact) to emphasize the grotesquely isolated faces of characters who are cut off from each other and from the world that exists in the darkness around them. Whether or not you notice the lighting immediately, be prepared to look for patterns of light and shadows. Are there important graphic patterns (such as sharp shadows) created to highlight a scene or a series of scenes in a movie? Does the lighting or coloring seem totally natural or unusually artificial? Some experimental films make the entire subject of the film the artistic manipulation of light, but any intelligent narrative movie will use lighting with as much a sense of its possibilities and purpose as a painting does (Figure 13) .

Mise-en-scène, then, is about the theatrics of space as that space is constructed for the camera. This use of space — how it is arranged and how the actors and objects relate within it — can generate exciting topics and commentary. The balance or imbalance that relates figures or planes in the mise-en-scène can sometimes say more about that action than the dialogue: for instance, is one character always positioned above another?

Figure 13. In *Close Encounters of the Third Kind*, spectacular lighting techniques and graphics are the heart of the movie.

is one character always in shadows? Likewise, in comparing two sets or settings, you might discover a theme that would otherwise not be noticed. Do catastrophes, for instance, occur only in the city or only on land? A cinematic mise-en-scène can be as complex as a theatrical mise-en-scène, and the film writer should aim for the same acuteness and subtlety demonstrated in the following analysis of the mise-en-scène (specifically the setting) in Buster Keaton's *Our Hospitality* (1923):

> *Mise-en-scène* functions, not in isolated moments, but in relation to the narrative system of the entire film. *Our Hospitality*, like most of Buster Keaton's films, exemplifies how mise-en-scène can economically advance the narrative and create a pattern of motifs. And since the film is a comedy, we shall find that the mise-en-scène also creates gags. *Our Hospitality*, then, exemplifies what we shall find in our study of every film technique: an individual element will almost always have *several* functions, not just one.
>
> Consider, for example, how the settings function within the narrative of *Our Hospitality*. They help divide the film into scenes and contrast those scenes. The film begins with a prologue showing how the feud between the McKays and the Canfields results in the deaths of the young Canfield and the husband of the McKay family. We see the McKays living in a shack and are left in suspense about the fate of the baby, Willie. Willie's mother flees with her son from their southern

home to the North (action narrated to us mainly by an intertitle). The main action begins years later, with the grown-up Willie living in New York. There are a number of gags concerning early nineteenth-century life in the metropolis, contrasting sharply with the prologue scene. We are led to wonder how this locale will relate to the southern scenes, and soon Willie receives word that he has inherited his parents' home in the South. A series of amusing short scenes follows as he takes a primitive train back to his birthplace. Here Keaton uses real landscapes, but by laying the railroad tracks in different ways, he exploits the landscapes for surprising and unusual comic effects. The rest of the film deals with Willie's movements in the southern town and in the vicinity. On the day of his arrival he wanders around and gets into a number of comic situations. That night he stays in the Canfield house itself, since the law of hospitality has made it the only safe place for him. And, finally, an extended chase occurs the next day, moving through the countryside and back to the Canfield house for the end of the feud. Thus the action depends heavily on shifts of setting that establish Willie's two journeys, as baby and as man, and later his wanderings around to escape his enemies' pursuit. The narration is relatively unrestricted once Willie reaches the South, moving between him and members of the Canfield family. We usually know more about where they are than Willie does, and the narrative generates suspense by showing them coming toward the places where Willie is hiding.

Specific settings fulfill distinct narrative functions. The McKay "estate," which Willie envisions as a mansion, turns out to be a tumbledown shack. The McKay place is paralleled to (contrasted with) the Canfields' palatial plantation home. In narrative terms the Canfield home gains even more functional importance when the Canfield father forbids his sons to kill Willie on the premises: "Our code of honor forbids us to shoot him while he is a guest in our house." (Once Willie overhears this, he determines never to leave.) Thus, ironically, the home of Willie's enemies becomes the only safe spot in town, and many scenes are organized around the Canfield brothers' attempts to lure Willie out. At the end of the film another setting takes on significance: the meadows, mountains, river banks, rapids, and waterfalls across which the Canfields pursue Willie. Finally, the feud ends back in the Canfield house itself, with Willie now welcomed as the daughter's husband. The pattern of development is clear: from the opening shoot-out at the McKay house that breaks up Willie's home, to the final scene in the Canfield house with Willie becoming part of a new family. In such ways every setting becomes highly motivated by the narrative's system of causes and effects, parallels and contrasts, and overall development. (Bordwell and Thompson 142–143)

COMPOSITION AND THE IMAGE

In any movie, it is the camera that films a mise-en-scène: when you watch a movie, you see not only setting, actors, and lighting but all of these elements as they were recorded and then projected. The composition of a scene through the film image is what distinguishes film from drama, and it is another important dimension of the movies that a writer should be able to discuss. When you watch a family video, you might first recognize a party with you and your friends. With a closer look, you might also comment on how the images, because of coloring, or angles, make some of your friends look taller or darker than they really are. In the same way, a film image may influence the way you see a scene or a character in that scene. The student who begins by writing "The scene had three characters" will seem less attentive and less perceptive than the student who begins, "The angle of the scene made the three characters appear . . . " This section considers terminology you can use to discuss these compositional features.

The Shot

The *shot* is the single image you see on the screen before the film cuts to another image. Unlike a photograph, a single shot can include a variety of action, and the frame that contains the image may move. One shot may show a cowboy at a bar and then magnify the figure as the camera moves closer. When the image switches to another position and point of view on the cowboy — say, from the opposite side of the bar — the film has cut to a second shot. In writing about film, you need to be sensitive to the two primary dimensions of the shot: its photographic properties and its moving frame.

The *photographic properties* of a shot are those qualities of the film image that are found in any photograph, plus the speed at which the scene is filmed. These would include: tone, film speed, and the various perspectives created by the image. *Tone* refers to the range and texture of the colors in a film image. A movie such as *The Wizard of Oz* uses a Technicolor scheme full of primary reds and yellows to suggest a fantasy world very different from the black-and-white Kansas. Many films by Wim Wenders, such as *Wings of Desire* (1987), use stark black-and-white tones because he feels those tones provide more realism than color.

Woody Allen tells the story of *Zelig* (1983) with intentionally grainy, black–and–white tones that make parts of his modern movie look like an old documentary. Ask if the colors are realistic; if they are not, why not? Is there a pattern to the way a film uses a particular color or group of colors? Does the film use colors symbolically, as Bergman uses red in *Cries and Whispers* (1973) to suggest both violence and passion? If the movie is in black and white, how does this add to it, especially when the filmmaker could have used color? How do the colors and tones relate to the themes of the film?

Film speed is the rate at which the film is shot; it is most noticeable in instances of slow or fast motion. Action in slow or fast motion usually indicates a change in the nature of what is happening or how the audience is supposed to perceive what is happening. Sometimes slow motion is used to indicate that the action occurs in a character's dream; sometimes fast motion is a way of commenting comically on a scene — when, for instance, the action on an assembly line suddenly moves at superhuman speed. It is easy to note when the speed of the film is no longer normal; be prepared to examine why these moments are singled out by the filmmaker. In Oshima's *Merry Christmas, Mr. Lawrence* (1983), David Bowie confronts his Japanese adversary with two kisses, which are filmed in slow motion; it is clear that this is Oshima's way of underlining a shattering climax in their relationship. Keep in mind, however, that many older, silent movies were filmed and printed at the rate of sixteen frames per second, and, depending on how they are projected, their action may look faster when shown at the modern standard of twenty-four frames per second.

The *perspective* of the image refers to the kind of spatial relationship an image establishes among the objects and figures it is photographing. These relationships are the products of different kinds of lenses and the way those lenses are used. Thus, one movie may constantly present scenes with *depth* or *deep focus,* so that the audience can see characters in the background as sharply as it sees characters in the foreground. Another movie (often an older film) may wish to isolate or highlight only certain characters or events in the image, and it consequently uses a *shallow focus* that will clearly show only one plane in the image, such as the man with a gun who stands in the foreground apart from the blurry crowd in the background. Much less commonly seen is the odd moment of *rack focus,* when the focus is quickly changed, or pulled, from one figure or object to another within the same shot, as when the image switches focus from the face of a man talking to a piano falling out the window in the background.

Still other kinds of perspective relationships can be used in creating an image, but even as you learn the technical terms, you can analyze perspective relationships by asking the basic questions. Who or what is in focus in an image, and why? Do the images create a world with depth, or does that world seem unusually flat? Does the space in a particular image appear crowded? open? wide? distorted? When a specific wide-screen image drowns the characters in space, what does this say about them and their world? Make the power of the image in itself come alive in your writing. Make the subject of your essays not just what you see, but how the image makes you see people and things in a certain manner and in a certain relationship to one another. Here is an example in which a student looks at color, tone, and spatial relations in Nicholas Roeg's *Don't Look Now* (1973):

N. Singerpanz

Don't Look Now is a movie about not wanting to see red but being unable not to see red. The story concerns a man and woman whose young daughter dies tragically by drowning. Later they go to Venice where he has a job restoring an old church, which is slowly sinking. They both want to forget the hor- rible death of their daughter, but in Venice they— and we, the frightened viewers—are pursued by a color, the bright red glow of the raincoat the daughter was wearing when she died.

Even before her death the color leaps out of the film. While the father is studying slides of the church he will repair, the tone and texture of the red in the image begins to vibrate and then ooze like blood. As if it is a premonition, he dashes outside to find his child face down in a pond, her coat the same color of the red in the slide.

Venice is a rather grey city in this movie, but wherever the father turns, the bright shade of red seems to catch his eye, as if it had a life of its own or was beckoning from another world. Stained-glass windows, pieces of clothing, or a passing car for a second or longer appear to be the shade of red which we and he have come to identify with the dead daughter. That red is a common color, if a shocking one, only adds to the mystery and confusion as this simple color grows more and more hypnotic and frightening. It seems to contrast with the ordinary grey life of Venice, and, since visual space is made so claustrophobic by the narrow, windy streets of the city, the glimpses we and the father catch of a fleeing red figure in the background become moments of true terror.

The color becomes a life in itself, a life that comes to mean death. The greys of Venice and the mazelike spaces of its streets make this color impossible to miss and more fascinating because it is always vanishing in the depths. The shock of the final scene, when we and the father finally corner the color, suggests that we have been horribly seduced by the power of Roeg's images.

The *frame* of the movie image forms its border and contains the mise-en-scène. Many movies, such as Jean Renoir's *Grand Illusion* (1937) and Hitchcock's *Rear Window* (1954) fill their mise-en-scène with the internal frames of windows or doorways or stage sets to call attention to the importance of frames and point of view in the story. Almost every film, though, must maintain a certain consciousness about the frame of the movie screen and the frame of the camera (Figure 14). A wide-screen frame is especially suited to catching the open spaces of a western or the vast stellar spaces of sci-fi films. The smaller standard frame is perhaps best suited for personal interior dramas or genres like the melodrama, for which a small frame can contribute to a sense of anything from domestic comfort and closeness to claustrophobia. In the course of watching a film, you will want to consider more particular questions about the framing:

- What is the angle at which the camera frame represents the action? Does it create a *high angle,* viewing its subject from above, or a *low angle,* viewing the action from below? When a conversation between two people is shot through a group of alternating high angles and low angles, it could mean that one character is tall and the other is short; it could also say that one of the two is the more dominant personality.

- Does the height of the frame correspond to a normal relationship with the people and the objects before the camera, that is, are they at eye-level, more or less? or does the camera seem placed at an odd height, too high or too low? At the beginning of *Rebel Without a Cause,* the camera is positioned at ground level to capture James Dean's desperate and pathetic embrace of a small toy as he crumbles to the ground.

Figure 14.   What makes this shot from *The Exorcist* (1974) disturbing?

- Does the camera frame ever seem unbalanced in relation to the space and action (called a *canted frame*)? If so, why does this occur when it does? Is it recreating the perspective of a character looking at the action from an odd angle, so that the buildings appear diagonal rather than vertical? Is it meant to recreate the perspective of a drunk, or might it be a more subtle way of commenting, say, on a community that lacks harmony and balance?

- What kind of distance does the frame maintain from its subject? Does the film use many close-ups (for instance, showing just the characters' faces), medium shots (showing most of a character's body), or long shots (showing full bodies from a distance)? Perhaps a scene uses a series of these shots, beginning with a long shot of a man on the street, following with a medium shot of him looking in a store window, and concluding with a close-up of his surprised face as he sees something in the window. Does the movie develop an elaborate combination of shots that might be interpreted within some meaningful pattern: close-ups for love scenes and long shots for battle scenes, for instance?

- Besides describing and containing the action, does the frame suggest other action or space outside its borders? Do important events or sounds occur outside the borders of the frame, in *offscreen space*? What is the significance of the offscreen space or its relation to what is seen within the frame? Is offscreen space used for comic effect, as in a Keaton movie in which we discover that the wheel he is sitting on is part of a train that is outside the frame and is about to move? Or does it have a serious meaning, as in Robert Bresson's films, in which offscreen space suggests a type of spiritual reality that his characters are unable to grasp or to understand because it is literally beyond the dimensions of their world?

Within one scene, any of these compositions could change as the camera creates a *moving frame* by altering its position in relation to the object being filmed. A romantic close-up of two lovers whispering, for example, may suddenly take on a new meaning when the camera frame moves backward and makes them part of a long shot full of spectators: what was at first romantic has become, through the movement of the frame, comic. This kind of framing action, called *reframing*, can be done in ways that rely entirely on the movement of the frame, not on the editing of images through cuts (see pp. 60–67).

When the frame moves to high, overhead *crane shots,* which look down on the action, we realize that there has been a dramatic change in perspective: the film might be emphasizing the smallness of the character in relation to the rest of his or her space, or it might be revealing other action, such as the approach of the cavalry on the far side of the mountain ridge. When the frame moves up and down, *tilting* from one position, this may simply be a means of following the point of view of a character who is looking up and down; it could also be a way of making a statement about high and low objects (about, for instance, the tourist who feels overwhelmed by the skyscrapers of New York City). Another kind of mobile frame is the *pan,* in which the frame moves from side to side without a change in the position of the camera or the point from which the scene is viewed: surveying the street before him, a character may look slowly from left to right, and the camera may pan to recreate the continuous movement of that gaze. In contrast, a *tracking* or *dolly shot* is not stationary but follows or intrudes on the action by moving the position of the camera (often moving along on tracks) and thus taking the frame forward, backward, or around the subject. During a cocktail party scene, a film may try to recreate the roving intimacy of the gathering by using a dolly shot that follows a character through the crowd. If this action were achieved by a *hand-held shot,* whereby the camera is carried by the camera operator, the shot might be jerkier and in some ways seem more realistic.

Since frames imply a perspective on the world or on certain characters, their mobility or a lack of it can point to the very foundation of the world you see in those frames. Is it an active world you are seeing or one that seems rigid and static? The complexities of that world will often be revealed as the frames move and change, and the more precisely you can note them, the more incisive your analysis will be. Try at some point to base your analysis of a character or a situation exclusively on the framing action that describes it. What patterns can you see? Does this character always look at the world through close-ups that track through crowds and situations, without getting a larger perspective on them? Does that consistent way of framing the action suggest that the character participates but never really sees the whole picture?

Remember that frames and their actions have no universal meaning. Just as colors do not have unchanging symbolic value, camera angles and movements do not necessarily mean the same thing in different movies. Low-angle shots do not always signify dominance, nor do high-angle shots always suggest oppression. Although in one movie a low-angle shot may remind the viewer that a weak character is seen by a stronger, more dangerous person, in another that low-angle shot may be used to describe the wonder of a child looking at a person she loves. If you begin by noting visual details carefully, you can reflect on how particular framing actions work in specific films and how they provoke questions about those films and their themes. An endless series of close-ups will mean one thing in a movie made for American television, where it may underline the importance of the individual character, and another thing in a European art film , where it could suggest the unknowable quality of the human face. In an Ozu film, the low height of the director's frame may be meant to suggest the more relaxed, meditative perspective of a Japanese looking at the world from the floor of a tatami room, but the Belgian filmmaker Chantal Akerman claims that the low height of her frames arises because she is short! The lesson should be clear: don't simply describe technical details and expect them to be self-explanatory. Rather, put them to work to convey an idea about the ways in which frames and their points of view operate and what they can mean in specific films, in specific cultures, and at specific times.

The Edited Image

In the simplest sense, *editing* is the linking of two pieces of film (two shots). Usually the editing follows some logic of development (an image of a woman, then the object she is looking at, for example) or aims to make a statement of some sort (an image of an egotistical czar followed by an image of a peacock). Recall the cowboy at the bar: when a long shot shows him at the bar and then slowly tracks in closer to capture him close up, this is reframing within a single shot. But if after that first image the camera stops and moves to another position (maybe a low angle on the other side of the bar), that reframed long shot has now been edited into two shots. The break between the two images is a *cut*.

A shot can be held on the screen for any length of time, resulting in a certain *editing pace* or *rhythm*. Since the pace of the editing is relative, we want to understand why and how a film or part of a film is edited according to a certain rhythm. We expect a chase scene to be rapidly edited, with lots of quick cuts and brief shots, but to make us comically aware of our expectations about editing, that chase scene could be edited with very slow rhythms and shots. As an exercise, observe exactly how long a single image remains on the screen in any movie, and then reflect on why the filmmaker cuts to another angle or image at that point. Does the director use mostly *long takes,* shots that remain on a scene or object for an unusually long time, as Terrence Malick does in *Days of Heaven* (1978) when he holds the image on the fields of grain for mystically long periods? Does the film cut rapidly from one image to another, as in the famous chase scene in *Bullit* (1969)? Does the pace of the editing change with the scene, for example, by using quick cuts on the streets and slow, long takes inside the home?

In the larger sense, editing, or *montage,* refers to how shots are built into larger pieces of a movie and hence larger units of meaning. A series of shots can thus be carefully joined to create a single *scene,* which is usually an action confined to one place and time: the interview between Tom Cruise and the college recruiter in *Risky Business* (1983), for example, or the scene in which the officers inspect the rotten meat in *Potemkin*. The latter begins with a group of angry sailors gathered on deck around a piece of maggot-infested meat; the ship's surgeon inspects the meat, which is shown in close up, and announces that the maggots are simply dead flies; the scene ends as another officer disperses the outraged sailors.

When these shots describe significantly more action and more time and more than one location, the interwoven and unified group of shots or scenes that results is often called a *sequence*. The entire party that surrounds the interview in *Risky Business* and the scenes that dramatize the sailors mounting discontent in *Potemkin* make those scenes each part of a complicated sequence. As part of the previous exercise, see if you can now mark off sections of a film that show how shots can be edited into complex relationships that create unified scenes or sequences.

Most of us pay little conscious attention to editing because we know and enjoy most the *continuity editing* of classical cinema. This editing style is appropriately called *invisible editing* because the filmmaker, not wanting the editing to distract from the story, avoids cuts and transitions between images that would be too obvious. Through various means, the filmmaker hides the film editing so that we view the images as a continuous picture. Thus, despite the fact that *The Maltese Falcon* (1941) is a carefully and stylishly edited movie — one that balances Sam Spade's entrances and exits and his keen method of noticing details in a room —

we view it as a continuous action in which obtrusive cuts would seem out of place.

Yet continuity editing depends on highly crafted editing techniques, techniques that, when analyzed, can reveal important points about the characters and the story. *Establishing shots* are those shots that begin a scene or a sequence as a way of locating it clearly in a certain place before dividing that sequence into more detailed shots. *Casablanca* (1942) begins with a series of establishing shots that describe the city on the map, the kind of people in the city, and finally, the outside of Rick's cabaret. Only then does the film move inside to begin its story about Rick. The *shot/reverse shot* pattern, or *shot/counter shot*, is another fundamental part of continuity editing. In this technique, an exchange between two characters (or a character and an object) is edited to appear logical and natural, by cutting from the person speaking or looking to the object or person that is being addressed or seen: for instance, a shot shows Bogart asking Ingrid Bergman a question, then cuts to her responding. When considering a film that uses continuity editing, a writer can begin, as with realism itself, by questioning the purposes of the techniques used:

- Are there larger implications in the continuity that concern the world and society? Does the movie try to create a sense of a logical or a safe world? Do establishing shots, for instance, indicate that the characters (and the audience) know where they are and should feel at home? Does the continuity help establish, as in *The Philadelphia Story* (1940), a sense of logical inevitability, the feeling that events and relationships have to move toward a natural conclusion, that Hepburn and Grant will marry?

- Has the continuity editing been adjusted to fit a genre or to create certain emotional responses? Do road movies have fewer cuts and more long takes? In Westerns, do the shot/reverse shot patterns involve people and things more than people and other people?

- When the editing presents a fundamentally continuous and unified world, are there times when that continuity is disrupted? Why? In *The Lady from Shanghai* (1948), Welles regularly disrupts the viewer's sense of space and time, through the questionable reliability of the narrator O'Hara or through visual distortions such as in the hall of mirrors at the end of the movie. In this case, the disrupting images and editing imply the collapse of a world incapable of maintaining the old certainties.

- Does the shot/reverse shot pattern in a particular sequence tell you anything about the characters or how they see the world and each other? Are considerably more shots given to one person or the other? Does the editing create a pattern in which one character's eyes never meet the other's?

- How would you distinguish between the continuity editing of an older, classical movie like *Ben Hur* (1925) and that of a more modern Hollywood film such as *Superman* (1978)? Does one use more long takes and the other more quick cuts? How would you differentiate between the continuity editing in a European movie like *Rules of the Game* (1939) and an American movie such as *The Grapes of Wrath* (1940)? Does the first rely more on a moving frame to emphasize the world that surrounds the characters and the second more on smooth editing techniques that emphasize the characters themselves?

Continuity editing can also use more noticeable and stylized methods, that are often associated with older movies. They include:

- *Fade-in* or *fade-out:* an image is darkened or lightened to make an image appear or disappear
- *Iris-in* or *iris-out*: a new image appears as an expanding circle in the middle of the old image, or the old image becomes a contracting circle that disappears into a new image
- *Wipe:* a line moves across an image to clear one shot and introduce another
- *Dissolve:* a new shot is superimposed briefly on the fading old shot

When these techniques appear in a movie, ask what they are meant to achieve. Used in older movies, these editing techniques created logical transitions from one time or place to another. In a Griffith film, a fade might be saying "later that same day" as the shot reveals the same kitchen in the evening; a wipe could suggest "in another part of town" — when the interior of the courthouse is wiped off by a line across the image and a Chinese opium den appears on the other side of the line. When watching an older film, ask if one technique is used for one kind of linkage (a wipe connecting two places, for example) and another technique for other situations (a dissolve indicating a change in time). In analyzing modern movies, ask why the editor would choose the older continuity devices. Does Woody Allen use irises just for humorous effect, since they are so unusual in a contemporary movie? In *The Cotton Club* (1984), are the wipes simply a reference to the 1920s, when the story takes place, or are they a dramatic means of emphasizing the passage of time and history — one of the main themes of the film?

Besides appreciating the techniques of continuity editing, you should learn to recognize, make sense of, and analyze how films undermine or challenge your expectations about continuity editing. Notice when a film, especially a more contemporary film, breaks with the standards of continuity editing, and ask these questions:

- Why are there so few establishing shots in a particular movie? Is it difficult to say where an action takes place because the scene begins with a close-up of a character or inside an unidentified room? Do the characters seem to share our disorientation? Is this disorientation related to the themes of the film?

- Why is the temporal continuity within a film broken up in such a confusing fashion? Does the editing use *jump cuts,* in which a continuous shot is suddenly broken and the image jumps to new figures or another background or even the same background at a different time? As a character discusses his life, for instance, the monologue may be broken in places, while the light in the room changes with each jump cut to indicate the passage of time. Is the filmmaker trying to make us more aware of the passage of time, or is he or she commenting ironically on this character's boring life story?

- Why is there no point of view we can identify with? Does this have something to do with the lack of shot/reverse shot scenes that would allow us to identify with the perspective of a character? Does the filmmaker, as Werner Herzog often does, force his audience to remain detached from ordinary people and to identify instead with animals, madmen, or dwarfs? Does the film contain images that seem to have no place in the story? A movie about war may inexplicably cut to an image of a cherry tree time and time again; is the tree a symbol? or a part of a character's memory? Why is the continuity of the action broken by this unexplained image?

In these cases the editing calls attention to itself, and the trade-off for that obtrusiveness is an initial confusion about why the editing upsets one's usual perception of the world. When that confusion leads you to larger questions (and perhaps to answers) about the themes and historical context of the film, you are developing an essay topic. After thinking about the Herzog movie, one student realized that his paper would discuss how Herzog's unconventional editing, particularly his undermining of a shot/reverse shot exchange, is part of an effort to move the audience outside the logical patterns that have traditionally placed human society at the center of the world, part of Herzog's vision of a natural world that is more important than individual men and women.

When examining editing strategies and the relationships between shots, begin with the following general guidelines and adapt them to deal with specific uses and variations in each film.

First, observe how the editing of the shots establishes relationships between objects and actions. Does the editing establish connections or oppositions among the people, things, and actions shown? In *The Last Laugh* (1924), the doorman is frequently linked to the image of the revolving door, and the identification of the two predicts the reversal of the man's good fortune. In *2001: A Space Odyssey* (1968), a prehistoric ape tosses a bone into the air, which then becomes the image of a spaceship. This famous *match-on-action* — two images edited together through a parallel action or motion — crystallizes thousands of years of human development propelled by violence and the need to conquer people and territory.

Second, accustom yourself to noticing abstract relationships between images. As the example from Eisenstein's *Potemkin* shows (pp. 27–29), the more abstract aspects of editing can be brilliantly used to achieve certain effects. Does the direction and movement of the figures in the successive images match when these shots are connected, creating, for example, visual and emotional force driving in a single direction? Are graphic contrasts or similarities created through the use of space in different shots, by alternating large and small spaces, for example? Does the editing produce certain rhythms by strictly controlling the length of each shot? (Although most of us know best the accelerated rhythms of a chase sequence, there are many other kinds of rhythms that the editing can fashion.) Remember, these formal patterns have no final and universal meaning in themselves, and their evolution through film history is not independent of historical questions. Although editing can be seen as a formal way of organizing images in time, there are usually more than just formal or technical issues involved here. Look precisely at editing, but let it lead you to think more about how and what films mean. In the following student essay, the writer examines a short sequence in *Citizen Kane* and relates the editing and the composition of the image to a specific theme:

Scott Richardson

Editing Breakfast in Citizen Kane

Soon after Charles Foster Kane marries Emily, the woman of his dreams who is brought back from Europe like one of his statues, their marriage begins to collapse. The severity and intensity of this collapse is captured in one two-minute sequence, which remains one of the most striking examples of Welles's evocative and economical editing in Citizen Kane.

The sequence begins with a medium two-shot of Kane and Emily in relatively warm light. Their conversation is teasing and intimate, visually reinforced by a shot/ reverse shot exchange of loving looks: he tells her she is beautiful, and when she complains about his having to leave for his newspaper office, he says he will call and change his appointments. That exchange is then followed by five more short shot/reverse shot pairs, and in each, the eyes of the couple grow increasingly suspicious and severe. The conversations are progressively hostile and clipped, and the newspaper becomes both a visual and verbal symbol of their growing division. In the first scene of this middle section, she complains: "Charles, if I didn't trust you. . . . What do you do on a newspaper in the middle of the night?" In the third, Emily pleads with him to stop

attacking her uncle, the President, in his newspaper.
By the fifth, he is not even allowing her to finish her
sentence:

Emily: Really, Charles, people have a right to
expect . . . .

Charles: What I care to give them.

Through the entire sequence, the changes in clothing and other aspects of the mise-en-scène also indicate that the passage of time is likewise a passage
from emotional intimacy. Kane changes from a romantic
tuxedo to a business suit. Their setting alters from an
unobstructed and close space to an obstructed space
cluttered with plants, flowers, and newspapers.

The succinct logic of the editing is then powerfully concluded with a shot/reverse shot and then
another two-shot. In the shot/reverse shot, the eyes no
longer meet or match, since they are now both reading
separate newspapers — he, his own (The Inquirer), she,
the rival (The Chronicle). Formally balancing the
opening of the sequence, the medium-long two-shot has
much colder and darker lighting. The two former lovers are
placed conspicuously at opposite sides of the frame.

The real time that this sequence describes is
probably many years. Yet, through a rigorous and
creative use of an edited space and a series of conversations within that space, Welles depicts more than
just the synopsis of a failed marriage. Linking the six
encounters, appropriately, with flash pans, he also
tells a succinct and cinematic version of the entire

```
tale of Citizen Kane: of how Kane's greatest desires
seem to turn to dust almost immediately after he
possesses them and of how he consequently becomes a man
always alienated in the great spaces that surround him.
```

SOUND

Few of us have learned to listen to the movies. What this common failure means to new and curious students is that many topics and problems having to do with film sound have only recently begun to be addressed and are waiting for good ears to take them up. If students with an interest in music and sound were to direct and concentrate that interest on a movie or a specific group of movies, they could tackle some original and provocative material.

In theory, sound can be used and edited with as much complexity and intelligence as images can. Certainly sound has many dimensions and uses in film: it can be described according to pitch, loudness, and timbre; it can figure in a film as *direct sound* (recorded when the image is being shot) or *postdubbed sound* (sound and dialogue added in the studio after the image has been shot). Movie sound can take the form of dialogue, music, or noise (thunder; a car screeching to a halt), with any or all of these sounds being naturally or artificially produced. Film sound can have a multitude of relations to the image and the narrative: it can be background music; its source can come from on or off screen; and it can precede or follow an image it is linked to (as when a character's remark forms a bridge into the next image).

Throughout film history one can find movies in which the sound alone would make a major topic for analysis. A well known example, Jean-Marie Straub and Danièle Huillet's *The Chronicle of Anna Magdalena Bach* (1968) sets up a complex opposition between the graceful music of Bach on the sound track and the tormented story of Bach's physical and financial troubles. Francis Coppola's *The Conversation* (1973) recounts the story of a man who specializes in sound surveillance, who tries to discover the truth through sound alone, and who finally loses all faith in the visual world. Some of the most fascinating and provocative uses of sound are found in films of the early 1930s, when sound was still being introduced into the movies. In one early sound film, *The Thirty-nine Steps* (1935),

Hitchcock employs sound as a central element in the plot: at a critical moment, he creates a dramatic *sound match* by connecting a woman's scream and the whistle of a locomotive, to link disparate images (Figures 15 and 16).

To write about sound, one must first learn to attend to sound — truly to listen. This does not mean that the more obvious or dramatic uses

Figure 15.

Figure 16.

of sound in film — in films with lavish soundtracks like Philip Glass's in *Koyanisquaatsi* (1982) or rock-concert films such as U2's *Rattle and Hum* (1988) — cannot make for good essays. But since a good essay is one that reveals intuitive, careful, and discriminating thinking, a good essay on sound will attend to what might escape the normal viewer and listener. A writer about sound in film might begin by asking bluntly:

- What is the relationship of the sound to the image in specific scenes or sequences? How might the answer to that question be refined to reveal the aims, achievements, or even the failures of sound in the movie?
- Is sound used to link images, or does sound have the conventional role of beginning and terminating with the image?
- Does sound ever become more important than an image, and what is the reason for this unusual strategy?
- Do the musical numbers in a musical have a special relationship to the narrative structure (for instance, do they occur when the characters need to escape into fantasy)?
- Why does the dialogue overlap or seem mumbled in some recent movies, making it difficult to understand the characters? Does the dialogue serve some other purpose than to help tell the story?
- What role does silence play in this movie?
- Are there sound motifs that identify characters or actions? Does the rhythm of the sound support or serve as counterpoint to the rhythm of the editing?
- If you had to pick three key sound sequences from this movie, which would they be and why?

These questions only sample the many inquiries that movie sound and particular movies might inspire. Listen to all film sound and write about it with the same curiosity and suspicion exhibited by the characters in Godard's *Everyman for Himself* (1980), who continually hear background music and wonder where it's coming from and why. Here a renowned French filmmaker and early innovator with sound, René Clair, writing in 1929, details one of the first successes with sound in the cinema:

> Of all the films now showing in London, *Broadway Melody* is having the greatest success. This new American film represents the sum total of all the progress achieved in sound films since the appearance of *The Jazz*

Singer two years ago. For anyone who has some knowledge of the complicated technique of sound recording, this film is a marvel. Harry Beaumont, the director, and his collaborators (of whom there are about fifteen, mentioned by name in the credit titles, quite apart from the actors) seem to delight in playing with all the difficulties of visual and sound recording. The actors move, walk, run, talk, shout, and whisper, and their movements and voices are reproduced with a flexibility which would seem miraculous if we did not know that science and meticulous organization have many other miracles in store for us. In this film, nothing is left to chance. Its makers have worked with the precision of engineers, and their achievement is a lesson to those who still imagine that the creation of a film can take place under conditions of chaos known as inspiration.

In *Broadway Melody,* the talking film has for the first time found an appropriate form: it is neither theater nor cinema, but something altogether new. The immobility of planes, that curse of talking films, has gone. The camera is as mobile, the angles are as varied as in a good silent film. The acting is first-rate, and Bessie Love talking manages to surpass the silent Bessie Love whom we so loved in the past. The sound effects are used with great intelligence, and if some of them still seem superfluous, others deserve to be cited as examples.

For instance, we hear the noise of a door being slammed and a car driving off while we are shown Bessie Love's anguished face watching from a window the departure which we do not see. This short scene in which the whole effect is concentrated on the actress's face, and which the silent cinema would have had to break up in several visual fragments, owes its excellence to the "unity of place" achieved through sound. In another scene we see Bessie Love lying thoughtful and sad; we feel that she is on the verge of tears; but her face disappears in the shadow of a fade-out, and from the screen, now black, emerges a single sob.

In these two instances the sound, at an opportune moment, has replaced the shot. It is by this economy of means that the sound film will most probably secure original effects. (93–94)

In observing and writing about any of these formal features, your first goal should be as much precision as possible. Developing a vocabulary of technical terms will be extremely helpful, but most important is developing the ability to write concrete descriptions of images and sounds in a way that best allows your reader to see and hear what you are describing. When you must work with only sketchy notes, try to get as much from those notes as possible. There is nothing wrong with writing about a general style ("a predominance of long shots" or "exaggeratedly artificial sets"), as long as your paper has a focus that justifies it. Otherwise, always try to integrate as much accurate concrete description as possible into your argument. As practice, describe — without analyzing — all the technical features of an opening or closing sequence of a movie or an especially interesting use of sound in a scene.

Interpretation, analysis, and evaluation are the primary goals of most writing about film today. Your appreciation of these elements of a film and how they work together must, at some point, be assimilated and made a part of your ideas about what the film or films mean. Whether you examine the editing of a sequence, the lighting throughout a series of films, or how the mise-en-scène, framing, and sound work together in a single scene, remember that seeing and thinking must join forces as you to put your perceptions into words.

SAMPLE ESSAY

This student essay on *Throne of Blood* (1957) is a good example of how a discriminating analysis can involve comparative questions (about film and drama) and, in the process, demonstrate how the movie uses specific technical manuevers to express its themes.

A Japanese Macbeth

A Japanese movie-version of Macbeth sounds like a bad idea until one sees Kurosawa's film Throne of Blood, in which Toshiro Mifune plays Macbeth. It is a much more satisfying film than, say, Olivier's Othello, largely because it is not merely a filmed version of a play as it might be performed on a stage, but rather it is a freely re-created version that is designed for the camera. The very fact that it is in Japanese is probably a great help to Westerners. If it were in English, we would be upset at the way some speeches are cut, but because it is in Japanese, we do not compare the words to Shakespeare's, and we concentrate on the visual aspects of the film.

There are several differences in the plots of the two works. Among the alterations are such things as these: Shakespeare's three witches are reduced to one; Lady Macbeth has a miscarriage; Macbeth is killed by his own troops and not by Macduff. But this paper will discuss another sort of change, the introduction of visual symbols, which the camera is adept at rendering, and which play an important part in the film. The four chief visual symbols are the fog, the castle, the forest, and the horses.

The fog, the castle, and the forest, though highly effective, can be dealt with rather briefly. When the film begins we get a slow panoramic view of the ruined castle seen through the fog. The film ends with a similar panoramic view. These two scenes end with a dissolve, though almost all of the other scenes end abruptly with sharp cuts, and so the effect is that of lingering sorrow at the transience of human creations, and awe at the permanence of the mysterious natural world, whose mist slowly drifts across what once was a mighty castle built by a great chief. The castle itself, when we come to see it in its original condition, is not a particularly graceful Japanese building. Rather, it is a low, strong building, appropriate for an energetic warrior. The interior scenes show low, oppressive ceilings, with great exposed beams that almost seem to crush the people within the rooms. It represents man's achievement in the center of the misty tangled forest of the mysterious world, but it also suggests, despite its strength, how stifling that achievement is, in comparison with the floating mists and endless woods. The woods, rainy and misty, consist of curiously gnarled trees and vines and suggest a labyrinth that has entrapped man, even though for a while man thinks he is secure in his castle. Early in the film we see Macbeth riding through the woods, in and out of mists, and behind a maze of twisted trees that periodically hide him from our sight. Maybe it is not too fanciful to suggest that the branches through which we glimpse him blindly riding in the fog are a sort of net that entangles him. The trees and the mist are the vast unfathomable universe: man can build his castle, can make his plans, but he cannot subdue nature for long. He cannot have his way forever, death will ultimately catch him, despite his strength. One later scene of the forest must be mentioned. Near the end of the film, when the forest moves (the soldiers are holding up leafy boughs to camouflage themselves), we get a spectacular shot; Shakespeare talks of the forest moving, but in the film we see it. Suddenly the forest seems to give a shudder and to be alive, crawling as though it is a vast horde of ants. Nature is seen to rise up against Macbeth's crimes.

Shakespeare's stage could do very little about such an effect as the fog, though his poetry can call it to mind, and it could do even less about the forest. Kurosawa did not feel bound to the text of the play: he made a movie, and he took advantage of the camera's ability to present impressive and significant effects.

Similarly, he made much use of horses, which, though
mentioned in Shakespeare's play, could not be shown on
the Elizabethan stage. In fact, in <u>Macbeth</u> (III. iii.
12–13) Shakespeare more or less apologizes for the
absence of horses when one murderer explains to the
other that when horsemen approach the palace it is
customary for them to leave their horses and to walk
the rest of the way. But the film gives us plenty of
horses, not only at the start, when Macbeth is galloping in the terrifying forest, but throughout the film,
and they are used to suggest the terror of existence
and the evil passions in Macbeth's heart. Shakespeare
provided a hint. After Duncan is murdered, Shakespeare
tells us that Duncan's horses "Turned wild in nature,
broke their stalls," and that they ate each other (II.
iv. 16–18). In the film, when Macbeth and his wife plot
the murder of their lord, we see the panic-struck
horses running around the courtyard of the castle—a
sort of parallel to the scene of Macbeth chaotically
riding in and out of the fog near the beginning of the
movie. The horses in the courtyard apparently have
sensed man's villainous plots, or perhaps they are
visual equivalents of the fierce emotions in the minds
of Macbeth and his wife. Later, when Macbeth is planning to murder Banquo, we see Banquo's white horse
kicking at his attendants. Banquo saddles the horse,
preparing to ride into the hands of his assassins. Then
Kurosawa cuts to a long shot of the courtyard at night,
where Banquo's attendants are nervously waiting for him

to return. Then we hear the sound of a galloping horse, and suddenly the white horse comes running in, riderless. Yet another use of this motif is when we cut to a wild horse, after Macbeth's wife has said that she is pregnant. In the film the wife has a miscarriage, and here again the horse is a visual symbol of the disorder engendered within her (the child would be the heir to the usurped throne), as the other horses were symbols for the disorder in her mind and in Macbeth's. All of these cuts to the horses are abrupt, contributing to the sense of violence that the unrestrained horses themselves embody. Moreover, almost the only close-ups in the film are some shots of horses, seen from a low angle, emphasizing their powerful, oppressive brutality.

Throne of Blood is not Shakespeare's Macbeth—but even a filmed version of a staged version of the play would not be Shakespeare's Macbeth either, for the effect of a film is simply not identical with the effect of a play with live actors on the stage. But Throne of Blood is a fine translation of Macbeth into an approximate equivalent. Despite its lack of faithfulness to the literal text, it is in a higher way faithful. It is a work of art, like its original.

(Reprinted from Barnet 265–270)

4

Six Approaches to Writing About Film

Two writers may be interested in the lighting in Fritz Lang's *Scarlet Street* (1945), but each may use a different method to focus the discussion: a formalist approach might mean analyzing the repetitions and variations of light and shadow within the film; a historical approach could involve showing how those lighting patterns can be linked with Lang's beginnings in the German Expressionist period. Likewise, different kinds of approaches are used when a writer discusses stylistic similarities in the films of Renoir or historical changes in the musical. In the first case, the writer would implicitly be using an "auteur" approach, which is based on the belief that films can be linked through the style of the director; in the second, the writer practices genre criticism, which presumes certain accepted types of movies. An awareness of these methods implies a more advanced intelligence in your writing than many competent writers about film might have (or even wish to have). Yet, even when you analyze a single film, it is important and useful to understand the approach you are using and the larger questions behind that approach, since this awareness will help you to identify the limits, the audience, and the goals of the essay.

As you consider an essay topic — such as an editing technique — and as you begin to give that topic shape, consider also the assumptions that consciously or unconsciously underlie your approach. Are you interested in a particular technique, such as parallel editing, because one director uses it regularly? Are you interested in examining a series of images because they relate the film to sociological and cultural issues, as Lotte Eisner does when she suggests that the many staircases in German films of the twenties relate to the romantic ambitions of the society of Weimar Germany? Do you want to focus on how the use of a technique, such as Eisenstein's montage, challenges the way editing has traditionally been used and thereby suggests an important change in film form? No matter what approach you find appropriate, it will always clarify your aims and limits to get a sense of the larger issues that underlie it. Comparing two films or parts of films, which is a common writing assignment, and deciding the terms of that comparison — formal, historical, or other — can be a first step in organizing an effective comparison.

The following introduction to the major approaches or methods used in writing about film does not attempt to review the complexities of any single approach or the ways two or more approaches can overlap in one study. These sketches and examples should, however, help you to identify approaches that can direct your writing about film and give you a sense of how a particular method might organize and use information in a distinctive manner.

FILM HISTORY

A historical approach is one of the most widely used methods in film criticism. It can be employed with varying degrees of emphasis or consciousness, but in general the writer using this approach organizes and investigates films according to their place within a historical context and in light of historical developments. Such an approach might explore:

- The relationships between films, as when a writer compares the use of sets in a film from the thirties with that in a film from the seventies
- The relationship between films and the conditions of their production, perhaps allowing a writer to make connections between American films of the eighties and the trend during those years toward the ownership of studios by large corporations like Gulf + Western or TransAmerica
- The relationship between movies and their reception, demonstrated in an essay that explores how television in the fifties changed the expectations of movie audiences of that time

While there are ways to write about film without emphasizing historical issues, some historical awareness informs most writing about film. An essay that examines *Mildred Pierce* (1945) in the context of post-World War II America and the changing sociological position of women would be based on a historical method, even though the direction and point of the argument may be a feminist critique. Similarly, an essay that presents a straightforward reading of the themes and style of *The Wild Bunch* (1969) could develop that reading by relating those subjects to the Vietnam War, to the history of the Western in American movies, or to innovations in movie technology during the sixties. Many exciting and informative historical essays have main topics that have little or nothing to do with the analysis of specific films and instead concentrate on historical facts and complexities — an economic crisis, say, or the political pressures behind an instance of censorship — which figure only indirectly in what an audience sees on the screen.

When using a historical method to help explain a film, beware of assuming that any movie, even a documentary, gives an unmediated picture of a society and a historical period. *Our Daily Bread* (1934) tells us a great deal about the early thirties and the American Depression, but what it tells us is bound up with historical questions concerning its style and intended audience as well as other historical issues. History is a delicate instrument; so use it with as much discrimination as possible. In *Film History: Theory and Practice,* Robert Allen and Douglas Gomery note that "doing history requires judgment, not merely the transmission of facts." In the following excerpt from their reading of F. W. Murnau's *Sunrise* (1927), they demonstrate how historical research can be used to fuel an initial curiosity about the lavish and artsy techniques of the movie:

> William Fox's decision to hire F. W. Murnau and to give him virtually carte blanche in the production of *Sunrise* involved much more than the addition of one more "highly artistic picture" to the 1927-1928 Fox schedule. Fox used Murnau's considerable biographical legend as part of a carefully orchestrated plan to elevate the status of his studio to that of preeminence in the motion picture industry. In the mid-1920s, Fox occupied, along with First National and Warner Bros., a middle echelon within the film industry both in terms of economic power and product prestige. *(Prestige* can be defined as the extent to which the films of a studio are perceived to be of "quality" in the critical discourse of the period.) In the mid-1920s Fox was known as a producer of unpretentious, "folksy" pictures, not highly regarded by critics but for the most part

popular with the mass audience. Examining the "Best Films" lists of *Film Daily Yearbook* and *Photoplay* for 1925, for example, we find that of 184 "best" pictures cited by 184 different critics, only 9 were Fox titles; in both lists the films of Paramount and MGM predominate.

In 1925, however, William Fox launched one of the greatest expansion plans in the history of the motion picture industry. The plan eventually collapsed with the stock market crash of 1929, but just before his downfall Fox controlled the production of Fox and MGM studios, Loew's Theatres, Fox's own large theater chain, and a one-third interest in First National Theatres, British Gaumont, and assorted other holdings. The Fox drive for economic power in the late 1920s was paralleled by attempts to enhance the prestige of Fox productions, and it is in this context that Murnau's hiring and his production of *Sunrise* must be viewed. Fox anticipated that Murnau's production of the highly artistic picture would bolster his studio's "special" films category. Unless the specials could attract greater critical attention, Fox would never have the prestige to match his hoped-for economic status. (99)

When you decide that yours will be a historical approach, ask yourself specific questions about the role history will have in your argument. Is the historical information you use background or introductory information for your study? Are you concerned with how and why certain historical events are represented as they are in the movie? Does historical background help explain narrative or technical maneuvers in the film? Does the movie stand out in history or is it part of a historical trend? Is your argument intended to clarify that place? What is more important to your argument, the historical facts behind the film or how its successive audiences responded to it, or both? No matter what your specific subject, ask yourself what part history might play in it.

NATIONAL CINEMAS

If historical issues usually play some part in essays on the movies, another important (and related) way to discuss them is in terms of their cultural or national character. The presumption behind this approach is that film cultures evolve with a certain amount of individuality and that to understand, for instance, the complexities of Dovzhenko's *Arsenal* (1929) one must locate it first in the political and aesthetic climate of postrevolutionary Russia. Similarly, to analyze an Indian film of Satyajit

Ray, such as *Distant Thunder* (1973), a writer should know something about the society and culture of India. According to this approach, ways of seeing the world and ways of portraying the world in the movies can differ for each country and culture, and it is necessary to understand the cultural conditions that surround a movie if we are to understand what it is about. An American spectator might have little trouble comprehending a Kurosawa film, but without guidance and some cultural background on Japanese society, the films of Mizoguchi or Naruse might seem too foreign and confusing for the average American student.

Observe how the author of the following passage identifies a group of Italian movies through a specific cultural heritage — their roots in the Italian neorealist movement and the later years of affluence in Italy — as a way of introducing her analysis of the films.

> A new group of filmmakers eventually emerged out of the growing power of Italian cinema, bringing to life an extremely heterogeneous and short-lived phenomenon referred to as the New Italian Cinema. Twenty years after the neorealist revolt, another angry generation appeared in the Italian film world this time not out of devastation and pain but out of the wellbeing of a consumer society. Their films were no longer full of compassion for suffering humanity; there were no attempts to capture "the tears shed by things." They were boiling with rage against a society that had developed during the past twenty years and against the older generation that had conformed to the rules — some of them well rooted in the fascist era — thus betraying, in the eyes of their children, the postwar ideals. Some of these new films were filled with explosive fury and utopian ideas already anticipating the events of 1968-1969. . . . (Liehm 188)

When deciding to discuss a movie or a group of movies from a foreign culture, a writer might begin by questioning, with an open mind, what distinguishes these films from the American films she or he is familiar with. (This implies that the writer will sketch a sense of what is specific about the American cinema of a given period.) How do the meanings of these films change when seen outside their culture? In what ways might you, as an American, understand British films of the fifties differently from the English audience of that time? What kind of cultural research might give you a better handle on the themes? Should you read something about the other arts, the politics, the economics of the movie industry there? Try not to simplify the connections between a culture and its films; remember that an approach of this kind implies (perhaps falsely) a unity or a fundamental similarity between many different films from a country. Could you find a similar kind of unity in American movies of the nineties?

GENRES

A French word meaning "kind," *genre* is a category for classifying films in terms of common patterns of form and content. Many of us casually practice the categorizing behind genre studies when we view movies: often we identify a set of similar themes, characters, narrative structures, and camera techniques that link movies together as Westerns, musicals, film noir, road movies, melodramas, or sci-fi films. Westerns feature cowboys and open, uncivilized spaces; sci-fi movies deal with adventures in outer space or intrusions by extraterrestrials. In analytical writing, some discussion of genre is frequently an effective way to begin examining how a film organizes its story and its audience's expectations. A Western such as Ford's *The Man Who Shot Liberty Valance* (1962) operates expressly out of a generic tradition, and although there may be many ways of talking about the film, one of the most important is to examine its subversion of the traditional patterns and expectations about the Western. This particular movie is the tale of a Western hero, but when we discover that this hero is not like the usual Western hero, we are surprised by the intentional generic variation. In the following passage, Andre Bazin begins his discussion of the genre by suggesting how *Stagecoach* (1939) perfectly assimilates other elements, like mythic motifs and the construction of the mise-en-scène, into larger generic patterns.

> By the eve of the war the western had reached a definitive stage of perfection. The year 1940 marks a point beyond which some new development seemed inevitable, a development that the four years of war delayed, then modified, though without controlling it. *Stagecoach* (1939) is the ideal example of the maturity of a style brought to classic perfection. John Ford struck the ideal balance between social myth, historical reconstruction, psychological truth, and the traditional theme of the Western *mise-en-scène*. None of these elements dominated the other. *Stagecoach* is like a wheel, so perfectly made that it remains in equilibrium on its axis in any position. (149)

In writing about film genres, always keep in mind questions of history, as Bazin does here, since genres change with the times; also identify for yourself the structures, themes, and common stylistic techniques of a genre. When did this type of movie first appear? What are its antecedents outside film history — novels, opera? How has it changed through history, and why? Does the story of the movie you are analyzing fit the genre it seems placed in? If not, does the mixing and matching of generic formulas serve a purpose, as in *Bladerunner* (1982), in which the detective and sci-fi genres, among others, are superimposed? As genres mature through the years, you may discover a strange self-consciousness in a film's use of generic formulas, as in *The Man Who Shot Liberty Valance*. How is this self-consciousness used? Is it an attempt to poke fun at the genre, or is it an attempt to show the limits of the genre in describing the complexities of the modern world — making a road movie like *Thelma and Louise* (1991), for example, a provocative variation on a genre dominated by male relationships?

AUTEURS

Auteur criticism is one of the most widely accepted and often unconsciously practiced film criticisms today: it identifies and examines a movie by associating it with a director or occasionally with another dominant figure, such as a star (say, Clint Eastwood). In a sense, referring to "a David Lean film" or "a Steven Spielberg movie" is in itself a critical act, since it implies that the unifying vision behind what you see on the screen is the director's and that there are common themes and stylistic traits that link films by the same filmmaker. Although a writer may refer casually to a dominant actor or even a screenwriter as an auteur (an "author"), auteur criticism has its historical roots in claims of literary independence and creativity made by and for certain directors. Since then, it has become a standard strategy in writing about film, with the director understood to be the auteur who anchors and unifies our perception of the film. Here, Thomas Elsaesser examines characters in the films of Samuel Fuller and pinpoints general character traits and actions attributable to Fuller's guiding vision and consistent interests:

> One of the most distinctive features of a great number of Fuller heroes is their willingness — indeed their compulsion — to expose them-

selves to situations charged with contradiction. The Fuller heroes, as it were, come to life only under conditions of extreme physical or mental stress; they seem, and often are, on the verge of hysteria, and their mode of action betrays a kind of electric, highly explosive energy.

Paradoxically, the impression one gets is that this apparent mental and emotional instability is what makes them strong in will and action. I am thinking of figures like the Baron of Arizona, Zack in *The Steel Helmet*, O'Meara in *Run of the Arrow*, Tolly Devlin in *Underworld USA*, and even Merrill in *Merrill's Marauders*. All live impossible situations, and knowing they cannot win, they nevertheless act with a kind of conviction, a kind of instinctive immediacy — as if they were engaged in an incessant flight forward, and were committing themselves to a course of action in whose perverseness they almost seem to rejoice, because they intuitively accept it as the fundamental condition of their existence. (291)

Although auteurism provides the foundation for many excellent studies, it should be used with some skepticism for at least two reasons. Rarely does a director have the total control that the term suggests, since anyone from a scriptwriter to an editor could be more responsible for the look and logic of a film. And what an auteur represents can differ quite a bit depending on the time and place; "auteur" applied to Truffaut or Claude Chabrol has quite a different meaning from "auteur" applied to Samuel Fuller or David Lynch. If you embark on a comparative study of the editing in two films by the same director, you should make it clear that you know you are using an auteur model and indicate how that tag applies to this director. Ask also how the historical conditions of film production encourage or discourage the auteurist unity you find in his or her work. Were the films made as part of a studio system, as were George Cukor's, one in which the influence of the studio might be more noticeable than the influence of the director? Or did the filmmaker have a great deal of independence, as does the British filmmaker Peter Greenaway, and thus significant control over how the film looks? What are the most distinctive signs of a filmmaker's control over the film: editing? the stories themselves? the themes? the setting? Are your expectations about a film conditioned by what you know about its director, as when you anticipate a great deal of violence from a Sam Peckinpah movie? Why? What kind of changes were there in the director's work over the years, and how do you account for them? Are there special marks of this filmmaker in each of the films, like Hitchcock's cameo appearances, Von Sternberg's cinematic portraits of Marlene Dietrich, or Spike

Lee's appearance as an actor in some of his movies? Keep in mind, finally, that sophisticated auteur studies are interested first in the films, not in the psychology or private life of the filmmaker.

KINDS OF FORMALISM

Formalism is a name given to film criticism concerned with matters of structure and style in a movie, or with how those features discussed in Chapter 3 (the narrative, the mise-en-scène) are organized in particular ways in a movie. In most instances, a writer will want to discuss these formal matters together with the major themes of a film, but the chief focus of these essays will be on formal patterns such as narrative openings and closures, the significant repetition and variation of camera techniques, or the relation of shots and sequences to each other. In the context of a discussion of CinemaScope and by concentrating on color and space, the writer of the following excerpt presents an illuminating and exact account of a sequence in formalist terms:

> In *Rebel Without a Cause* (Ray, 1956) a shot of extraordinary beauty comes after the first twenty minutes of the film, during which the surroundings have been uniformly cramped and depressing, the images physically cluttered-up and dominated by blacks and browns. Now, James Dean is about to set out for school; he looks out of the window. He recognizes a girl (Natalie Wood) walking past in the distance. Cut to the first day/exterior shot, the first bright one, the first "horizontal" one. A close shot of Natalie Wood, in a light-green cardigan, against a background of green bushes. As she walks the camera moves laterally with her. This makes a direct sensual impression which gives us an insight into Dean's experience, while at the same time remaining completely natural and unforced. On the small screen, such an image could not conceivably have had a comparable weight. (Barr 10-11)

Strictly speaking, formalist criticism does not emphasize matters outside the film proper, such as the different effects a movie can have on audiences, the historical conditions of its production, and other questions that are not immediately apparent on the screen. Rarely today, however, do you find an essay that is purely formalist; usually a formalist analysis becomes part of other arguments about an auteur, a film history, a genre. A purely formalist analysis might therefore investigate narrative unity in

His Girl Friday, in which the two main characters propel the plot along through a series of confrontations and crises that begin in their divorce and end in their marriage. One writer may look for stylistic or formal repetitions in the editing or lighting of a movie and then describe how it works in relation to the rest of the film. Another option is to choose a visually complex scene or sequence and describe how it works and why it is important to the movie. Early in *Shane* (1953) there is a quick and involved exchange of looks among Shane, the farmer, the wife, and the child, an exchange that sets up social relationships for the remainder of the movie; a formal analysis might explain how the camera communicates so much so quickly. Whether you are examining a single shot or a pattern of images, ask yourself what is most interesting and significant about the formal features and how they add to the story and themes. Is it the mise-en-scène that appears most crafted, or is it a series of camera angles? If you concentrate on a single scene or sequence, how do the sound, lighting, and camera movement interact to comment on or support the action of the story? How would you relate the formal features of the film to its themes?

IDEOLOGY

In one sense, "ideology" is a more subtle and expansive way of saying "politics," at least when we think of politics as the ideas or beliefs on which we base our lives and our vision of the world. Ideology might refer to one person's belief in the sanctity of the family or to another person's sense that civilization is basically progressive. When we see a movie such as *Red Dawn* (1984) or *Potemkin*, there is little chance of our mistaking the political messages at work: the first proclaims the threat of Communism to America, the second hails the force of a socialist revolution. Less obvious, however, may be the messages about life and society communicated in films such as *Rocky* (1976), *Porky's* (1982), *The Sound of Music* (1965), and *Dances with Wolves* (1990). Like the majority of movies, these films present themselves as entertainment, and their makers would probably resent any claim that unintended social or political perspectives are at work here. Yet most of us would probably acknowledge that each of these films offers rather clear ideological messages about individualism, gender relations, the importance of family life, race, or American history.

Similarly, many of us might see *The Godfather II* (1974) as an exciting, well-made gangster film, but a writer sensitive to the ideological values in the movie might see those elements as part of another perspective, one concerned with the business of capitalism:

> *Godfather II* clearly shows the destruction and/or unobtainability of the basic bourgeois values. They are not destroyed because they are inadequate *per se;* family ties, social mobility, quest for security, male companionship, and even religious values all relate and correspond to real universal human needs for community, love, respect, support, appreciation. Coppola demonstrates that the social institutions — nuclear family, Mafia family, ethnic community, and the Church — upon which the Corleones relied to provide and protect these values withered before the irrational, destructive forces of capitalism, the main goal of which is profit, not the meeting of human needs.
>
> Coppola builds up, interweaves, and finally destroys four levels of familial affiliations — the nuclear family, the Mafia family, the ethnic community, and the Catholic Church. Through careful juxtaposition, he shows how each strives unsuccessfully to create an ideal community. In all cases, the needs of business destroy whatever communal aspects these associations might provide. In fact, it is the very effort to conserve and support these families that becomes corrupted by business and destroys them. *Godfather II* works out on the level of human relations Marx's insight that capitalism, even at its best, must destroy human life and associations to exist. Thus, the more vigorously bourgeois society strives to achieve the ideals it has set for itself, the more destructive and corrupt it becomes. And this contradiction is most clearly visible in American gangsterdom, the perfect microcosm of American capitalism. (Hess 11)

In critical writing attuned to ideology, any cultural product or creation carries, implicitly or explicitly, ideas about how the world is or should be seen and how men and women should see each other in it: the clothes you wear express social values just as the films you watch communicate social values. Whether we agree or disagree with the values expressed in a particular movie, the ideological critic maintains that these movies are never innocent visions of the world and that the social and personal values that seem so natural in them need to be analyzed. Good writing of this kind usually avoids the obvious politics of propaganda in a movie like *The Green Berets* (1968), where the American presence in Vietnam is naively hailed, and instead looks into the more subtle or troublesome manipulations involved in films like *Terms of Endearment*

(1983), in which the presentation of women is much less progressive than it at first seems. (In this kind of analysis, the intentions or claims of the filmmaker should not necessarily be accepted as an indication of what the movie is truly about.) The best examples of ideological criticism avoid limiting themselves to the content of a movie; instead, sophisticated ideological criticism will relate questions about characters and plot to more complex points about the shape of the narrative or the distance of the camera from the characters: what, for instance, is the ideological point of a war movie in which the enemy is seen only in large groups or in which the camera makes them all look alike?

With an ideological approach, begin by pinpointing the message or messages that a film aims to communicate about its world and, by implication, our world. What is it saying explicitly? What is it saying implicitly? What does the film suggest about how people relate or should relate to one another? Is individuality important? Is the family important? Is the film straightforward and direct about its values and what they demand, both gains and losses? Are these values depicted as "natural," and if so why? Does the movie challenge the beliefs of its audience or support them? Why? How do the politics of the film and the way it entertains intertwine? Particularly with issues related to gender and race, ideological criticism today offers many exciting ways to look at movies: how movies depict women or minorities, how movies exclude people of color, how movies are seen by audiences outside the middle class. Above all, ideological approaches urge you to be suspicious of what you might normally take for granted.

As you read and write more about film, you will encounter other approaches to writing about film to add to the list of principal approaches described in this chapter. And you will find that these approaches overlap and can be used with various degrees of emphasis depending on what you wish to say about the movie. Writing about a film by Jan Kadar would probably involve the writer in questions about Kadar's status as an auteur, his place in Czech and American cinema, and both the historical and formal features of his films (a short or even a medium-length paper is not likely to allow this much scope). You should consequently never be too restricted by a particular approach, nor should you hesitate to work out other ways to write about film. Yet knowing these models and being conscious of when you may be using them can be valuable in organizing your thoughts and in bringing your writing into focus. Most important, recognizing different ways of looking at the movies and writing about them will enable you to choose which method or methods best suit your own interests and aims.

SAMPLE ESSAYS

The first essay, written by a knowledgeable film student, examines Fritz Lang's *M* primarily as part of a tradition of German cinema and within the larger context of German culture and politics of the early thirties (Figures 17 and 18). Observe, however, how formalistic questions and auteurist assumptions also play a role. In the second essay, a student who began only with an uneasy feeling about a film's portrayal of women demonstrates an ideological approach to *Ordinary People* (1980). More precisely, her essay is a feminist reading of the movie: it is less concerned with what the film intends to say than with what it does say about how women appear in a male-dominated society. Her "reading against the grain" of the film nonetheless remains very close to the images and actual story.

Figure 17. "The normal man-on-the-street becomes a menacing reflection of himself" (*M*).

Figure 18.   The mirror-images of *M*.

M. Trillo

The title is a
specific and
accurate des-
cription of the
paper's content.

The opening is
general but
engaging.

The Reflection of M:
Germany as a Culture of Crisis

Fritz Lang's 1930 M is a suspenseful and
horrifying tale of a psychotic child-murder.
Its technical accomplishments alone make it
worthy of attention: an economic and imagina-
tive use of sound, sophisticated cross-cutting
editing, and graphic compositions which are
sometimes as detailed and evocative as paintings. Because of these accomplishments, M will
probably always appeal to audiences of different generations and from many different coun-

tries. But, for my purposes, Lang's film is most intriguing as a reflection of a turbulent German society in the early thirties. Whether consciously made in this way or not, <u>M</u> seems to work as a mirror-image of the rise of fascism in Germany, but in reflecting that rise the film may be most important as an attempt to expose it to the German audience that was so involved in fascism and its growth.

German culture in the twenties and early thirties was, as is well known, caught in a crisis. The gradual collapse of the Weimar Republic from 1919 to 1933 created a society that seemed to live in a kind of chaos or disorder, a chaos that was economic, social, and psychological. Poverty, unemployment, and depression became widespread realities, and the stable sense of a personal identity once found in a German tradition and a very ordered society seems to have been destroyed by the catastrophic defeat of World War I. This general disorder and instability is reflected in many of the major cultural trends of the period. The nightmarish dream paintings of Edvard Munch are the very influential emblems of a whole school of German Expressionist artists whose focus was on the dark turbulent world beneath the quiet surfaces of everyday life. Freud's writings also became more and more important during this period, which is especially appropriate since

Margin notes:

A question or problem is stated —

which leads to a clearly announced and focused thesis.

A brief but pertinent discussion of cultural and historical background.

The background material is related more specifically to artistic traditions.

his work discusses the dark unconscious below men and women's conscious life and also sketches a civilization full of secret discontents

(Willet).

The German Expressionist Cinema of the twenties was likewise concerned with this crisis and its depiction. As Siefried Kracauer and Lotte Eisner have shown, some of the most important movies made during this time depict a "haunted screen" reflecting much of the unstable reality of the society. From The Cabinet of Dr. Caligari to Nosferatu, the Vampire, many of these films seem regularly to be about madness and destruction, and even in the realistic "street films" the settings and plots describe a world that is collapsing into ruin. In the tyrants and madmen that often control the chaos in these movies, many viewers have seen the foreshadowing of Hitler, the Caligari who would step in to use the insecurity of the crisis as a vehicle for massive destruction (Kracauer, Eisner).

These motifs are central to M, which draws from that Expressionist tradition in which Lang himself worked during the twenties. The central character Becker (Peter Lorre) is a man possessed by something he cannot control, a mad compulsion to murder children. Beneath his

---

Margin notes (left column):

The source for much of this information is cited.

The cultural and historical context is further focused on two key film movements, highlighted with references to particular films and two scholarly sources. Throughout this paragraph, the writer reminds his readers of the original title and thesis ("the crisis"). "Likewise" becomes a useful transition word.

The first sentence works as both a transition ("these") and a topic sentence, pointing to the analysis of the single film in question. Very short summary of the film's central theme.

placid and calm exterior and in the midst of
everyday life, the insane killer begins to
throw the world into disorder. Stylistically,
the film draws on both the Expressionist and
the "street realism" tradition of German film.
The insanity is shown, on the one hand, in a
number of expressionistic shots, like the
spiraling staircases that indicate entrapment

Still focused on the film, the writer connects formal and stylistic questions to the larger culture and social history. "Conversely" connects discussion of two German film traditions that inform the movie.

and a dizzy lack of perspective. Conversely,
there is the street realism of social poverty
and underworld life which gives M a kind of
documentary look at times. Unlike some Expressionist films, it should be noted, it is difficult to distinguish in M between the dream
world of psychological chaos and the social
chaos of the street. Or, to put it in terms of
the story, Lang makes it difficult in this
Post-Expressionist movie to say whether Becker
is an evil madman or a victim of some force
that runs through the whole society.

Topic sentence reasserts central thesis and introduces analysis. Specific, concrete examples are described, along with the precise technical detail from the film.

The movie makes this confusion and the
crisis it implies fairly explicit at times. The
balloon, which becomes the symbol of one of
Becker's victims, has a pudgy human shape, and
its resemblance to Becker's shape might suggest
a connection between the killer and the victim.
The law and order of the police who search for
Becker are, through Lang's parallel cross-
cutting, identified with and almost indistin-

guishable from the underworld crime mob that searches for Becker too. Lastly, there are the carefully orchestrated mob scenes (as during the final trial) which nonetheless appear as hysterical and bloodthirsty as the pathetic murderer seems. (At these instances, I can't help but think of the murderous actions of the Nazis in the name of law and order or of the perfectly ordered crowds of soldiers who became the machines of war.)

A personal reflection is inserted — one that intelligently expands the themes of the film.

There are then a number of double images or double reflections in M that seem to muddle the questions about a society in crisis. Where does the crisis originate? Where is the order and where is the disorder? What is the nightmarish dream and what is the reality? This double image and the questions it provokes are most apparent in the character of Becker, specifically in the number of times that he and the audience are made to examine his image. Frequently Becker examines himself and sees himself in mirrors, searching out the madman that exists somewhere inside him. At one point, Lang shows Becker looking in a shop window, where the image of Becker is contained in a frame within the film image—a frame made by a reflection of knives laid out in a diamond shape inside the store. Here, the normal man-on-the-street becomes a menacing reflection of him-

A transition and summary ("There are then"), which then moves to the central point of the essay: mirror-images.

More concrete description that attends both to what is seen and how it is formally presented.

self. Later, Becker discovers he has been found out and exposed by seeing a reflection in another mirror-image which reveals the tell-tale "M" on his back.

What the reflections expose in these different shots and scenes is not exactly the same thing. Yet, in each, it is the dark side, the disorder, the murderous impulses of self (and society) that is sought out and discovered. In most of these mirror-images, furthermore, the camera places the audience at an angle so that it seems to participate in that reflection—either looking over Becker's shoulder or directly into the reflection itself. Just as the film builds up a strange sympathy for the madman Becker, these mirror-images seem to force an audience to view its own darker side in the reflecting images of a psychotic killer.

If <u>M</u> is then, like other German films of the late twenties and early thirties, an indirect reflection of a German culture in crisis, it is also more than a simple reflection. Combining the two traditions of Expressionism and street realism, it makes nightmares real and reality a nightmare in a manner far more disturbing than most other German movies of the time. Perhaps this is what the German authorities recognized when they forced Lang to change the original title "A Murderer Among Us" because they

The writer expands his analysis of certain themes and formal strategies (the crisis contained in the "mirror-images") to describe how the images on the screen address and challenge the audience.

Some further summary that condenses (but doesn't repeat) the argument.

A dramatic broadening of the main points of the essay, but this time in terms of the history of the filmmaker, the auteur behind the film.

thought it was too politically sensitive. When Lang fled Nazi Germany a few years later, he probably reaized, however, that no movie, even one as powerful as M, would be enough to stop the tyrannical darkness that was surfacing in the streets of Germany.

Works Cited

Eisner, Lotte. <u>The Haunted Screen</u>. Berkeley:

Univ. of California Press, 1969.

Kracauer, Siegfried. <u>From Caligari to Hitler</u>.

Princeton: Princeton Univ. Press, 1947.

Willet, John. <u>Expressionism</u>. New York: McGraw-

Hill, 1970.

A title that succinctly but explicitly indicates an argument or engagement with the main theme of the movie.

The opening paragraph introduces a common understanding about what the film means, then moves quickly to state the writer's alternative "point of view." Concentrated in the final sentence, the thesis and argument are focused further by relating them specifically to the main character, Conrad.

The topic sentence recalls the thesis but shifts its emphasis to the centrality of male relationships and the isolation of women.

The negative characterization of the mother is dramatized specifically in terms of her actions in the kitchen — a

Marcia L. Ferguson

The Not-So-Ordinary Women
of Ordinary People

Ordinary People is intelligently acted, well scripted, and critically and financially successful. It is apparently an "honest" look at upper-middle class America, presented as an impartial record of one family's emotional turmoil and ultimate collapse. Yet, seen from another perspective, this supposedly honest and impartial movie can be viewed as a careful construction of women as agents of disaster or failure. When examined from this point of view, we see that women in Ordinary People are consistently seen and shown from a male perspective in which they function mainly to devastate and disrupt the already shaky state of the film's protagonist, Conrad Jarrett.

Male bonding pervades this movie but is always overshadowed by the threat of invidious females, especially the chilling character of the mother Beth. The force of this threat isparticularly evident during the daily rituals of eating, that domestic sphere traditionally controlled and orchestrated by women exiled to the kitchen. Around and within these eating rituals we best see the subtle violence and manipulation on the part of the mother. Early in the film, for example, Conrad struggles to dramatic, visual space that allows the writer to integrate details of the editing, dialogue, and the composition of the images.

return to "normal" life after his suicide attempt and subsequent stay in a mental hospital. A casual call from his father to come to breakfast panics Conrad, and a swift sequence of shots interweaves his distress and the mother's efficient, machinelike preparation of food. By the time he enters the kitchen, looking ill and nervous, we are his visual comrades, flinching along with him at the painful

The author repeats words like "normal" and "ordinary" to remind us that these ideas, as they are depicted in the movie, are the very notions that this paper questions.

tension within the breakfast ritual: while the dialogue remains superficially ordinary, the quick editing between faces and actions makes it clear that breakfast with this mother is anxiously violent. When his mother serves him french toast and tells him it is his favorite, he quietly says he is not hungry, and without a word she whisks the plate away before a close-up shows her viciously stuffing it down the garbage disposal. The father and son can only react with bewilderment to this unpredictable female, who in this early scene is already established as less balanced than the skittish son.

More concrete detail, important to support an argument that critiques the "intended" meaning of the film. Note that incidents from the film are

When it is obvious that the family breakfast has been destroyed by the mother, the father Calvin tries to save the situation by suggesting that Conrad bring his male friends home to "play touch football on the lawn." His attempt to rescue one ritual with another is more used not simply to recount what happened but to support an idea and an interpretation.

exactly an attempt to replace female trouble with male bonding. Calvin invokes a whole team of males to replace the shattered scene resulting from the mother's punitive violence. At this point in Ordinary People, however, her presence is far too strong, and the reunion of the father and the son must be delayed through a full series of narrative encounters and revelations.

A strong transition is made from the previous paragraphs with the phrase "asserts itself again."

Technical and stylistic evidence, described precisely.

The mother's presence asserts itself again shortly after the breakfast scene, this time in a dinner scene vividly underlined by the stylistics of the film. The scene opens with a medium-long shot that gradually tracks in through a dining room doorway. The shot is rigidly balanced as the frame of the doorway lines up perfectly with the sides of the film frame, and the dining-room table is in the gradually opening center of the frame. The mother is at one side of the table, Conrad at the other, and the father in the center. Within this balanced frame and the commonplace conversation, Conrad seems safe. The mother begins, though, to press him about his "torn shirt," and he immediately shrinks from her gaze. When he answers another demanding question by saying he hasn't played tennis in a long time, Beth snaps back, "Well, don't you think it's time you started?" appearing unusually threatening and tall as the camera holds on her from a low angle for a noticeably long time. In the background of the shot is the father looking small and uncomfortable; the rapid cutting and close-ups emphasize that the original balance of the scene was merely delaying the fragmentation it at first disguised.

The writer continues to alternate the two key points in her argument about "male bonding" and female disruption. At the same time, she depicts this as a *developing* problem that the film's narrative will work to solve.

Calvin again attempts to bond with his son in the wake of the mother's aggressive attack (which is exactly how this "ordinary" moment is portrayed). He asks Conrad the name of his female friend from the hospital, a person whom the audience knows is important to Conrad. Beth then immediately announces her implicit control of the scene by leaving the table as if to abandon the distasteful topic (and probably the competition of another female). From that point on she is physically absent from the table yet

More excellent visual detail, made lively by varying sentence structures with different kinds of subordinate phrases and positions.

very much in control as she oversees the two males from the back of the shot. Knowing this, they exchange silent but meaningful glances, the only real communication the camera so far allows them while under the tyrannical eyes of the mother.

A major expansion of the argument claims that the crisis the mother represents is part of a much larger problem with women in the film.

These examples do not, it must be emphasized, describe simply a tale about one bad woman and mother. All the females in Ordinary People are inept; all women fail Conrad. His meeting with Karen, the friend from the hospi-

tal, is, despite its promise, especially disappointing. She carefully denies the friendship
they formed at the hospital by concentrating
the conversation (appropriately in a restaurant) on her new appearance of normalcy and her
adjustment to an "ordinary" world. A school
play is much more important than any intimacy
she and Conrad may have shared in the hospital:
"That was the hospital; this is the real
world." She exudes a cheerfulness and enthusi-
asm that Conrad's troubled spirit cannot match,
and in many ways she seems to be becoming a
replica of Conrad's mother interested only in
appearances and unable to respond to male
"substance."

The theme of
normalcy and
the ordinary
returns.

Even the most redemptive female character,
his newly found girlfriend Jeannine, ultimately
abandons him. Again at a restaurant, she tenta-
tively reaches out to him by asking him about
his suicide attempt. He responds by saying she
is "the first person to ask" such a question,
and he begins to answer her in what appears to
be the first therapeutic act of communication
in the movie. Just then they are interrupted by
a rowdy group of males (mostly the athletes who
describe another theme in the film); she reacts
by giggling and allowing them to pull her from
the table, thus destroying the potential bond
between her and Conrad, who is visibly shaken

The argument about the problem with women is expanded through the significance of Conrad's girlfriend, who represents "weakness" in the name of propriety.

by the incident. In the logic of this scene, she is clearly the one who has failed Conrad after he opens up to her, and later she tries to explain it by saying she laughed out of embarrassment at being singled out by a group of males. In effect, she, like the other females in the movie, sacrifices Conrad to a so-called feminine sense of propriety.

Sharp transition from the weakness and propriety of the female characters to the need for the male characters to separate themselves from that world in order to be reborn in male camaraderie. The first part of the paper described the suppression of that bonding; this section describes how that bonding can be rediscovered by rejecting women.

In Ordinary People, this sense of propriety becomes aligned with a feminine weakness that is seen best in the subplot of the father's rebirth as a man. In his conversation with a business partner (both jogging athletes), he regrets his inability to fire incompetent female secretaries who "crack gum in your face." And, when he turns to Conrad's psychiatrist while looking for a way to deal with his wife's coldness, he comes away from this new male bond realizing how weak his wife has made him by dominating him with her femininity. (She made him change his shirt the day of their son's funeral because it didn't look right.) The father discovers that he needs to be strong, that he no longer loves his wife because she may be "beautiful" and "unpredict-

Phrases of dialogue are inserted into the writer's sentences to make the point.

able" but is "not strong, not giving." Conrad discovers, through the same psychiatrist and his confrontation with the "weak" suicide of Karen, that he has superior strength, which is why he survived the boating accident. That strength is what finally allows the men to banish the weak and destructive mother, and with her departure the men are free to bond in a male embrace.

Ordinary people are therefore men who are strong but do not know it and women who fail those men by not allowing them to bond as men. In the ordinary style of this movie, the two-shot of men communicating together becomes the longed-for goal of the movie (attained at the conclusion), and in one of the most revealing scenes in the movie, when the father prepares to take a snapshot, a two-shot, of mother and son, the mother refuses to participate. The point is obvious, even if unintentional: if an intimate two-shot with a male is the test of an honest reality, in Ordinary People women are clearly excluded from it and the reality it represents.

A concise summary of the argument crystallizes the point in a single scene and shot.

5

Style and Structure in Writing

Perhaps the greatest temptation and the most common danger in writing about film is to approach your material as if you were simply "at the movies." Describing and analyzing what you have seen as if it were the subject of a casual conversation or a "sneak preview" for a friend or classmate will not result in an effective and polished piece of writing. Good writing on any topic is improved by a relaxed style, but the lure of film's immediacy should not distract you from the care and preparation that a film essay requires.

When a viewer confronts a movie using the various approaches and the critical vocabulary discussed in the preceding chapters, the actual writing of an essay can be considerably easier. Any anxiety about finding ideas and arguments should be relieved if one methodically takes this central step.

In *Day for Night* (1973) Truffaut comments on the inevitable gap between the grand conception of a film and the nuts-and-bolts execution of that plan (Figure 19). Writing about film is similar. In both instances, the final expression of our ideas involves adjustments and work that, as Truffaut suggests about his movie, may change and even improve the original conception. This means that the tools for executing the writer's ideas — in this case, the principles of effective writing — must be attended to with the same care that the writer took to conceive of those ideas. We have all seen movies that are based on a brilliant idea but fall flat because of poor technique. Writers should be wary of making a similar mistake.

If you have taken good notes, you will have gone a long way in the "prewriting" stage. The next most crucial element of the essay is a clearly focused topic — a thesis — that will allow you to engage the film or films from a workable angle. This will also permit you to do a thorough analysis

Figure 19.   The nuts and bolts of composing an idea in *Day for Night*.

in a limited number of pages and, at the same time, expand along lines broad enough to keep your reader interested. Even if your instructor presents you with a general topic, you will usually have to refocus it in a more specific, personal manner. Discussing racism in D. W. Griffith's *The Birth of a Nation* could prove too large a task for a ten-page paper. Conversely, an essay focused on a truly minor detail, such as the use of blackface in that movie, could prove too trivial for a long essay unless handled with dexterity and developed through research.

The scope and focus of your essay will depend, as we have noted, on the audience you foresee for it. An informed audience will not be interested in a familiar plot or such elementary knowledge as "Griffith was an American filmmaker." The sooner a writer determines the audience, the sooner the parameters of the essay will start to take shape. This is a critical step in writing about film because much of what you say and see, particularly during a second screening, is guided by those parameters.

Another central task of the first stage of writing is *outlining* your topic. Many skilled writers do not work with an outline, finding it too constricting. Others find outlining absolutely necessary, especially because of the fleeting nature of a film. Under the best circumstances, a writer sketches out an outline while organizing notes into a coherent point of view on the film. An outline can take any form, ranging from a list of main points to a formally numbered and sectioned blueprint of an argument, complete with headings and subheadings. Outlines provide real assistance with the logic of an argument. A clearly thought out outline can be invaluable when you view a movie for a second or a third time: it becomes a kind of view-finder that enables you to spot significant details missed on the first screening. Here, in one student's outline for a paper on John Sayles's *Brother from Another Planet* (1984), the writer uses full sentences to make certain that complete ideas define the main sections of the argument:

Sue Raines

Strangers and Brothers in John Sayles's

<u>Brother from Another Planet</u>

I. This is a science-fiction movie, but it is primarily about racism.

II. It uses a variety of themes and techniques from the sci-fi genre.

   a. some themes

   b. techniques and style

III. The problems of being an alien from another planet become identified with the problems of being a racial minority.

   a. appearance

   b. language

   c. victimization

IV. In the end, the movie is about more than racism; it is about being "strange" and the hope that all "strangers" might unite as "brothers."

```
a. other strangers and oppressed in the movie

b. conclusion: how to rediscover the planet

   earth
```

When the paper is written it will probably depart from this outline, and it will certainly become more defined and more specific. Yet, an outline of any kind provides a foundation on which to build.

THE RIGHT WORDS

Concrete Language

The actual writing of the essay involves guidelines that are basic to all writing and are important to rehearse and recall frequently. Since a film critic is recreating a film and a perspective on it through language, a sensitive and accurate use of words is paramount. Concreteness is the heart of some of the best film writing, largely because the reader depends so much on a visualization of a scene or sequence. Also, the accuracy with which a writer describes what he or she sees is often the most convincing way to make a point. After seeing a striking sequence from Werner Herzog's *Fata Morgana* (1970), an inexperienced writer might be tempted to write, "There were a series of strange shots, with crazy dialogue and odd characters." An experienced writer, like the author of the following passage, revitalizes the images with a lively and concrete idiom in order to comment on them:

> The strongest sequence may be a catastrophic metaphor of hell on earth: a catatonic drummer and a tacky female pianist on a tiny stage in a brothel perform a piece they have played a thousand times without any emotion, endlessly, off-key. "In the Golden Age, man and wife live in harmony," the commentator says, as they are photographed head-on, with all the merciful cruelty of a humanist filmmaker who must show everything. At the end of the piece, they remain immobile. There is no applause. (Vogel 76)

Denotation and Connotation

Denotation and connotation are rhetorical tools that can be used effectively or ineffectively by a writer. A *denotation* is the dictionary meaning of a word, and thus "film" and "movie" have the same denotation. If you mean "sequence" don't say "shot"; if you mean "Hollywood style," don't be satisfied with "classical style," since the latter could indicate a specific kind of Hollywood or European movie. Be precise: say what you mean and avoid words that have little denotative value, like "thing" and "aspect."

A *connotation* is any association or implication of a word. "Film" has for many people sophisticated, intellectual connotations, while "movie" has connotations associated with mass entertainment. Both "Hollywood" and "classical" carry a number of connotations that a writer should be aware of ("commercial" or "establishment," for instance). Mack Sennett, the founder of the Keystone Cops, warned against inappropriate critical language when he said there was "a wonder and a miracle" in his films that "no amount of expensive grammar can explain."

Tone

The tone of an essay can vary considerably from the jaunty sarcasm of some newspaper reviewers to the pretentious didacticism of some film theoreticians. *Tone* is the total effect of the words you use and how you use them, and every essay establishes a tone or a "writer's voice." Be conscious of the tone of voice you are adapting in your argument; some tones are less appropriate than others. Sarcasm, humor, and anger are among the least effective tones to use in formulating an engaging and convincing argument. A paper that begins "This so-called art film could never appeal to a normal audience" immediately identifies the writer as someone too prejudiced to make balanced judgments. The same point could be made with a more formal tone: "The problem with art films is that they can alienate a public used to a more accessible story." A writer needs to find the right compromise between casual voice and formal voice. The nature of that compromise will depend on you and the specific topic of your essay. Too much slang won't work, nor will pretentious words that you normally never use. A writer conscious of tone will maintain a consistent one throughout the essay, not changing from sentence to sentence or paragraph to paragraph.

Beware of using quotation marks around words to create an indirect or "clever" tone or sarcasm. When you want to say that a character behaves like a dominant and oppressive male stereotype, don't be satisfied by writing that he is a "really liberated" guy. Quotation marks used in this way rarely explain anything; they usually only blur your meaning.

Repetition and Clichés

A common challenge in word usage is to keep one's diction fresh and varied. Experienced writers rely on the *repetition* of key words for emphasis and continuity. But the lazy or uncontrolled repetition of words makes for tedious prose: repeated references to "the director" throughout a short passage can be irritating. Such repetition can easily be varied by substituting a proper name ("Romero") or an article ("he"). When you find yourself locked into unnecessary repetitions, vary your descriptions and phrases. But don't force a change by using terms that do not fit your style.

The tendency to depend on *clichés* is a version of the same problem: the substitution of a quick and unexamined use of language for precise expression. The snatches of jingles and pat quips that we often find in movie reviews are an extreme version of this use of clichés. They indicate how meaningless terms like "blockbuster" or "a film everyone should see" can become.

In the following passage, Robin Wood employs expressions we have all heard before ("very much in question," "a great pity that"), and he builds his point around the repetition of words like "energy," "ridiculous," "artist," and "violence." Here, however, Wood demonstrates how common expressions can contribute to a relaxed tone and how the repetition of a word can sometimes lead to finer distinctions in thought.

> The value of Sam Peckinpah's work is still very much in question; its intensity is not. And art that expresses such energy and passion, such commitment to personal impulse, commands, at least, respectful attention. *The Wild Bunch* (1969) and *Straw Dogs* (1971), whatever one's estimate of them, have that combination of candor and force which announces an artist who is not afraid of appearing ridiculous; those who profess to find them no more than ridiculous are perhaps nervously insulating themselves from the films' ferocious and contagious energy. At the same time, one may comment at the outset that it is a great pity that, in the eyes of the public and most critics, Peckinpah's gentler and arguably finest films . . . have been so overshadowed by the spectacular and explosive violence of the more notorious works — a violence that is certainly a major component of his artistic personality, but by no means the whole story. (771–772)

EFFECTIVE SENTENCES

Economy

A writer should aim at two key stylistic goals: to be economical and to be interesting. Being economical means saying precisely all that you need to say and cutting words and expressions that add no information or serve no stylistic purpose.

Many writers can get stuck for words and are unable to come up with sentences that adequately express a thought. When this happens, going back to an outline and talking through your ideas in terms of specific images and sequences will help start the flow of sentences. The inverse problem can be equally troublesome: sometimes a writer who spews out words in haphazard fashion loses the meaning of his or her sentence in the process. A critical eye notices that the following sentence is unnecessarily wordy:

> There are many difficult and demanding scenes in this film by Lina Wertmüller, <u>Swept Away</u> (1975), which give the movie an operatic quality.

Cutting and economizing, the writer would revise it to:

> Lina Wertmüller's <u>Swept Away</u> is a demanding, operatic film.

Wordiness of this kind can usually be eliminated by watching out for redundancies, wordy constructions ("there is"), avoidable instances of passive voice ("Blake Edwards directed *The Pink Panther*" is shorter and more effective than "*The Pink Panther* was directed by Blake Edwards"), and words that could be deleted without changing the sense of a sentence. Reviewing the following passage, the writer should have recognized its extreme wordiness:

> Despite its central and obviously important role in

```
the way a movie communicates, one of the most over-
looked and ignored areas of study in film scholarship
is proving to be the many varieties and appreciable
differences in how movie dialogue has been used and how
its functions have changed rapidly through history and
dramatically from director to director.
```

Without sacrificing information, the revised, more succinct version reads:

```
Despite the central role of film dialogue, most
scholarship has overlooked its evolution in films
and its various uses by different directors.
```

Varied Sentence Structures

An interesting style requires more than just an interesting subject to write about. It also requires a way of presenting the subject in sentences that dovetail and emphasize your material in the strongest way possible. Holding a reader's interest — always a goal of any writer — requires sentences that present your analysis in the most effective form. Some authors seem to "shoot from the hip," naturally and chattily presenting their points in a lively fashion. Most of us, however, tend to get stuck in stylistic ruts, of which the most common in student writing is the unvaried use of simple declarative sentences. In order to escape these ruts, we use several stylistic strategies that make our sentences more flexible and emphatic. Parallels, coordination, and subordination are three of the most important.

Parallels draw attention to the relations between, or the equation of, two or more facts or ideas:

```
Hollywood movies have three purposes: to entertain,
to make money, and to advertise a way of life. (not
". . . to entertain, to make money, and advertising
a way of life.")
```

Coordination joins two related sentences with a conjunction (and, but, or), resulting in a compound sentence and rhythmic variation in your sentence patterns:

```
Hollywood movies are meant primarily to entertain
and make money, and, less obviously, they aim to
advertise a way of life.
```

Subordination combines two or more points or sentences into a single complex sentence that redistributes those ideas to deemphasize some points and emphasize others:

```
Although Hollywood movies aim to entertain and to
advertise a way of life, their primary function is
to make money.
```

In the following passages, the writer has gotten stuck in the repetition of sentence structures, and the writing is choppy and tiresome:

```
Ingmar Bergman is the premier Swedish filmmaker. He
has been active in film and theater since 1944. His
most famous movie is probably The Seventh Seal
(1956), and this film dramatizes typical Bergman
concerns with theological and social angst. His most
visually complicated film is Persona (1966), and it
examines that angst as it relates specifically to
images, personalities, and the cinema.
```

Revising these sentences, the writer communicates the material more effectively and economically through the use of parallels, coordination, and subordination:

```
Active in film and theater since 1944, Ingmar
Bergman is the premier Swedish filmmaker. Although
```

The Seventh Seal is his most famous movie, his most
visually complicated is Persona; while the first
dramatizes typical Bergman concerns with theological
and social angst, the second examines that angst as
it relates to images, personalities, and the cinema.

In making these sentences a bit more economical, the writer has made them more emphatic: in the first sentence, by subordinating less important information about Bergman's past; in the second, by creating parallel phrases that compare the two films and by subordinating the less interesting *Seventh Seal*. The original sentences could have been restructured in many ways. Their structure will be determined not only by economy, but by what the writer wishes to emphasize.

Many improvements in style are not made in a first draft. When you are composing a first draft from notes and reflections, it is probably best not to labor over finding the exact word or the most economical phrase. At that stage, your objective is to get your ideas down on paper as quickly and as completely as you can. The time for correcting and polishing sentences comes when you revise that draft, when you should be more sensitive to how you can improve your writing.

COHERENT PARAGRAPHS

In a movie, the elements that compose a mise-en-scène (actors, props, etc.) become part of a shot; many shots develop into a scene and then a sequence; and sequences can be combined to form a narrative. The growth of an essay can be conceptualized according to a similar scheme. Perhaps the logic of writing is never quite so schematic, yet, just as an accurate and resourceful use of words leads to lively sentences, well-constructed sentences become unified and coherent paragraphs.

There is no set length for a good paragraph, nor is there a correct number of paragraphs for a given paper. A 500 word essay normally has about four or five paragraphs, and a developed paragraph usually contains at least four or five sentences. However, the number of paragraphs and their respective lengths will depend on the ideas presented in your argument. Ideally, the number of paragraphs in an essay will follow from a thorough and well-conceived outline. If you have only two or three paragraphs, or very short paragraphs, your argument may be short on good ideas or your ideas may not have been thought out fully or supported concretely. (Although journalistic writing, such as a newspaper review, frequently uses very short paragraphs, this is usually *not* the kind of paragraphing appropriate to a critical essay.)

Whether the paragraph has a few sentences or a dozen, there must be an idea that clearly unites the sentences in the paragraph. This unifying idea should be made explicit in the *topic sentence* of each paragraph, a sentence that pinpoints the guiding concept of the paragraph. When you locate this sentence at the beginning of a paragraph, you help the reader to follow the train of thought throughout the paragraph. At times your topic sentence will appear as the second sentence. Rarely does a paragraph come at such a point in the essay that a topic sentence is unnecessary, and in most cases you should not use, in place of a topic sentence, a *plot sentence* that simply retells some of the plot. Generally, a topic sentence anchors the paragraph and announces its central idea, even when that idea will be developed through two or three other, related ideas. Note in the following paragraph how the central idea ("the repose of the Western hero") is clearly identified in the first sentence. Note also how the author creates a smooth transition from the previous paragraph about the gangster film through the appropriately placed "by contrast."

> The Western hero, by contrast, is a figure of repose. He resembles the gangster in being lonely and to some degree melancholy. But his melancholy comes from the "simple" recognition that life is unavoidably serious, not from the disproportions of his own temperament. And his loneliness is organic, not imposed on him by his situation but belonging to him intimately and testifying to his completeness. The gangster must reject others violently or draw them violently to him. The Westerner is not thus compelled to seek love; he is prepared to accept it, perhaps, but he never asks of it more than it can give, and we see him constantly in situations where love is at best an irrelevance. If there is a woman he loves, she is usually unable to understand his motives; and he finds it impossible to explain to her that there is no point in being "against" these things: they belong to his world. (Warshow 137)

Here characteristics of the Western hero are described separately: his perspective on life, his breed of loneliness, his feelings about love and violence. Each, however, can be referred to and is subordinate to the central topic of his "repose." As with most good paragraphs, this one features a general and clear beginning and then moves through specific points to a strong and emphatic conclusion.

The next example of paragraphing has a more complicated structure. Note its successful use of transitions ("In more general terms," "yet," "however") to connect parts of sentences, separate sentences, and separate paragraphs:

> In terms of sound quality, the average film of the mid-forties, whether in Hollywood, France, or England, represented a significant improvement on the original efforts of the late twenties. In more general terms, however, the films of the forties remained the direct descendants of those earlier films. Every step of the process had been improved — from microphones to printers, from amplifiers to loudspeakers — yet the fundamental optical recording and printing technology remained basically the same. Not until after the war, thanks in part to German wartime technology, did the sound recording industry in general and the film sound track in particular take a quantum leap forward with the perfection of magnetic recording techniques. As with all important technological developments, however, the magnetic recording revolution met with immediate economic resistance. There was no question that magnetic recording was easier, used lighter, more mobile equipment, cost less, and produced decidedly better results; theaters, however, were not equipped to play films which substituted a magnetic strip for the traditional optical sound track. Just as Hollywood delayed the coming of sound for years, it has for economic reasons delayed the coming of better sound for decades. Over a quarter of a century after the general availability of magnetic recording technology very few theaters (usually only the high priced, first run, big city variety) are equipped with magnetic sound equipment. Ironically, for years, the average amateur filmmaker working with super-8 sound equipment has possessed better and more advanced sound reproduction facilities than the neighborhood cinema.
>
> Nevertheless, Hollywood was able to capitalize on the new technology in another way. Though filmmakers around the world continued to use optical sound for distribution prints, they very early began to do all their own recording in the magnetic mode (by the end of 1971, 75 percent of Hollywood's original production recording, music scoring, and dubbing was being done on magnetic recording equipment). Finishing what the playback had begun, magnetic recording divorced the sound track still further from the image and from the image's optical technology. Now, any number of sound sources could easily be separately recorded, mixed, and remixed independently of the image (thus simplifying the manipulation of stereophonic sound now often coupled with the new wide-screen formats). (Altman 48)

These are rather complicated paragraphs, in part because a great deal of information is proffered, in part because more than one idea is at work in the first paragraph. Specifically, the writer is discussing two ideas like a kind of two-sided coin: on the one side are the advances made in sound technology until the mid-forties and postwar period (announced in the opening sentence); on the other side is the failure of Hollywood to implement those advances.

The author balances and contrasts these two developments by mapping the logic of their progression from the prewar period to modern times, and he connects them through key transition words like "however." Notice also how this back-and-forth progression is deftly focused in the middle of the paragraph with the sentence beginning "There was no question": this sentence has a parallel structure, its two halves divided by the colon, each side representing a version of the twofold point the paragraph makes. Also, the coherence and vividness of the paragraph is enhanced by concrete details and historical facts. (When writing papers more analytical than historical, this kind of information may not be as necessary, available, or appropriate. But always attempt to solidify and flesh out the idea of your topic sentence with hard facts or concrete details from the film.)

Finally, the passage demonstrates a neat transition between the two paragraphs that turns on the word "nevertheless" and the phrase "in another way." Make sure your transitions between sentences and between paragraphs add clarity, coherence, and fluidity to your essay. Using words or phrases specifically suited for this purpose, like "furthermore" or "in fact," is one way to increase coherence; a second method is to repeat key words from the end of the previous paragraph, as this writer does with "Hollywood" and "technology." Always make sure that your reader has a logical transition to follow from one paragraph to the next.

INTRODUCTORY PARAGRAPHS

Many of us — like Alvy Singer, who in *Annie Hall* refuses to enter a movie theater even a few minutes late — know how important a beginning is. Although many Hollywood films settle quickly into mediocre stories and styles, the first ten minutes can provide the most captivating and innovative sequence of the entire experience (which is one way of keeping you in your seat). Beginnings are crucial to any presentation, and, no matter how long your essay will be, getting that first paragraph right could be the most important revision of your essay.

An essay must hold a reader's interest if it is to communicate information or make a point, and the introductory paragraph is where that interest should first be piqued. Starting your paper with a string of commonplaces — that Frank Capra was an American director, that his films were very popular, and so on — is not likely to encourage your reader to continue reading. Even when a reader (say, your instructor) is obliged to finish reading an essay with a dull beginning, that first paragraph creates an expectation about your work. The first paragraph is the ideal place to give your reader a clear sense of your topic and how you intend to develop it — the *thesis statement* that sets out exactly and specifically the argument of the essay. Even in a long and ambitious essay, that direction is clearly announced as a signpost and provocation for the reader:

> In the late 1930s, public discussion about Hollywood changed. Clergymen in backwater towns could still raise a crowd by railing against sin on the silver screen, and judges and reformers here and there continued to maintain that movies led impressionable youth to crime. Among academics and in literary circles, however, and in the principal newspapers and magazines, the moviemakers were regarded with considerably more respect, awe and even envy, as the possessors of the power to create the nation's myths and dreams. (Sklar 195)

The essay's title, "The Making of Cultural Myths: Walt Disney and Frank Capra," catches the attention of many readers who recognize both names but would not necessarily place them on common ground. As with all good openings, however, the introductory paragraph does not simply restate the title ("This essay will discuss cultural myth in the movies of Walt Disney and Frank Capra"). Instead it introduces its topic in terms that are more general and at the same time more concrete. Starting with a specific historical reference (the late thirties), the paragraph describes a specific historical transition in the debate between those who thought the movies were frivolous and those who believed they were an important cultural medium. With that debate as a background, the paragraph moves to its thesis about the power of the movies of Disney and Capra to create social myths.

NOTE: Whether you formulate a title before you begin writing a first paragraph or after you have finished a final draft, always make the title an informative and enticing entry into your first paragraph: it should be broad enough to suggest the scope of your topic but specific enough to interest your reader. "Cultural Myths" would have been far too general a title for the last example; "Walt Disney and Frank Capra" would have been too quirky and unclear.

An opening paragraph should identify the object of study (here, moviemakers of the late thirties) and the topic the writer is focusing on (here, history and cultural myth). Often the focus is the analysis of a particular film or part of a film. You can organize a first paragraph by moving from a general proposition to a specific statement of your argument. Or, as the last example shows, you can move from specific examples to a more general thesis (but not too general!) that your paper will develop.

Introducing a provocative quotation or a specific image is one way to energize a first paragraph. Whatever method you use, your aim is to convince your reader immediately that you have something worthwhile to say, an argument that needs airing, observations that are not readily apparent. Although the rest of your paper will develop and expand on these first propositions, you should make very clear here what your essay is about and what method you will use to investigate your topic. If you compose and focus this paragraph to fit the length and limits of your paper, that paper will be much easier to write: nothing is more common and more disastrous than the massive thesis statement ("This is a study of *Terminator* (1991) . . . ") formulated when a writer doubts that he or she can find enough to say about a more narrowly focused topic.

In many ways, the first paragraph is the most difficult of the essay; it presumes that you know pretty much where the argument is going, although some conclusions are often arrived at in the writing itself. While it is important to formulate an introductory paragraph in the first draft, you should plan to reexamine and rewrite that paragraph once a later draft is done. At that point, an effective first paragraph will become much easier to write.

CONCLUDING PARAGRAPHS

For some students, a popular strategy for reaching a conclusion is to rephrase the opening thesis in slightly different words ("Thus I have shown . . . . "). This approach, however, frequently seems mechanical and dull. A concluding paragraph, like an opening paragraph, is best when it makes your reader attend to it, sit up and realize that something interesting has been said that may have implications beyond the bounds of the essay. Some summary is not necessarily a bad idea, especially when an argument has been a bit complicated or involved; even so, earlier ideas should be retrieved not merely to remind the reader of what has been said, but to emphasize a final point, as Dudley Andrew does in this conclusion:

> Thus, despite its apparently hermetic form, *Diary of a Country Priest* situates itself in a cosmic openness. It is a film written across the pages of a notebook, yet it is set in a field of light and sound. The concentration and discipline of the diary allow the curé to attain in his final hours a breadth of soul explicitly measured against his pathetically liberal defrocked friend. His rigorous instrument of self-knowledge — his writing — has brought him into focus with his image and, therefore, has made him one with Christ. It is through a similar textual discipline, this time of cinematic style, that Bresson can in the end reach beyond cinema and be at one with *his* subject, a novel. By going beyond cinema through cinema, he has achieved a revolution in the ethics and potential of adaptation; he has *performed* a novel in sight and sound, not capturing his subject so much as becoming it. (130)

Conclusions often attempt to wrap up too neatly a complex argument. Yet sweeping generalizations are risky. Some of the most effective conclusions will close an argument within the range of the essay, while at the same time opening it to other questions.

In concluding a discussion of Leni Riefenstahl's films and photographic work, Richard Meram Barsam moves carefully from the specific to the general, referring to historical figures and titles, arriving at definite conclusions about the woman and her work, yet maintaining a relatively balanced and open-minded tone that points the reader toward other questions:

> The Nuba film will be similar to her other work because it will express again the special world that has engaged her imagination since she was a child. Leni Riefenstahl's world is a world apart, a world of crystal grottoes, of men who think they are supermen, of the human body made godlike through film, of elite warriors on a dark and foreign plain. This world exists in fact, but it becomes in her imagination a very different entity. Protected by her belief in that entity, which is, of course, her art, Leni Riefenstahl remains apart from much of the everyday world. She cannot understand why many people in that world will not accept her or

her legends; as she publishes her Nuba photographs (to some, a bold and striking act of penance), she thinks that these documents will show her belief in man's honesty, goodness, and oneness with nature. The Nuba photographs do show those aspects, of course, but they are photographs of a disappearing world. Fortunately for all mankind, her photographs of Hitler represent another world that has disappeared, but the world will not forget that she found it necessary, and perhaps even advantageous, to make those pictures and to create the myths that infuse *Triumph of the Will* with its terrifying power. A truly enigmatic woman, Leni Riefenstahl fights against the legend that she has created for herself, fights against it even as it encloses the final years of her life. Leni Riefenstahl is one with her legend, inseparable from the world that she has made. She has what every artist since Daedalus has dreamed of, except the power to fall, to admit error, and to transcend the fragile barrier that stands between art and life. (37)

For some, the final rhetorical flourish here might seem a bit much. But conclusions and openings are always more rhetorical than other paragraphs, and, whether one chooses a matter-of-fact tone or not, writers should strive to get as much out of their words as possible, especially at the crucial points of an essay.

GRAMMAR, PUNCTUATION, PROOFREADING

While watching a movie, we all get annoyed if we see the sound boom appear in the frame or discover some unintentional lapse in the continuity editing. Sloppy inattention to detail distracts us from the merits of a work and lowers our opinion of it. In the same way, a failure to attend to the mechanical details of writing can cripple the effectiveness and strength of any argument, no matter how good it is. Like the movies, writing is in large part what it looks like: appearance is crucial.

A review of basic grammar and punctuation is beyond the scope of this book. Remember that *most readers will presume you know proper grammar and punctuation, and they will have little tolerance when they find blatant and abundant errors*. If you have difficulty with grammar and punctuation, you must take time to review the rules.

Always proofread your writing carefully. Allow enough time to set the paper aside for at least a day so that you can review it with fresh eyes for typos and mechanical errors. When time is short or if you have difficulty proofreading your own work, ask a friend to read the essay for obvious mistakes in the writing or typing. If your friend gives you more substantial help, you should acknowledge it in a note.

Ideas are communicated in their presentation. Like a film projection that is badly framed or has a defective sound system, a first paragraph riddled with mechanical errors makes it unlikely that you'll hold the attention of your audience for long.

CHECKLIST FOR WRITING AN EFFECTIVE ESSAY

Each writer has personal methods and strategies. The following are summary guidelines, suggestions, and reminders.

1. Be prepared for a movie. Before you see a film, ask preliminary questions about when and where it was made and about your own expectations concerning it. Ask which of your other interests — technology, art, business — might point you in a good direction when writing about film.

2. Learn to look carefully at the movie and to take notes. Let your general, preliminary questions become more specific as you respond to the movie. What seems most important in it? What seems most unusual about it?

3. Let your questions lead you to a manageable topic that involves both the themes of the film, and its technical and formal features. A topic like "The Search for Identity in *Citizen Kane*" is probably too large for a short essay; a much more compelling topic would be "Kane's Childhood: The Beginning of an Identity Crisis." The more concentrated focus of the second topic will allow you to examine scenes and sequences in detail.

4. Try to view the movie at least one more time after you have decided on a topic. Expand your notes at this point, filling in details you may have missed during a first screening.

5. Keep clarifying your argument; transfer your notes to note cards that you can arrange and label according to ideas that will help to organize your essay. Begin your argument with a statement of the problem or question you intend to address. Then as-

semble and lay out the specific points of your discussion using concrete evidence from the movie and your interpretation of it. Good essays usually proceed from the less debatable thematic points to more complex points about style and technique. Remember that you are presuming you have a reader who has seen the movie but will need to be convinced of whatever point you wish to make.

6. Many writers find it useful to sketch out the organization of an essay in outline form. Depending on your habits and preferences, the outline can be very complete and detailed or rather general and sketchy. If you tend to have trouble with organization and paragraphing, you will want to make it as complete as possible. For each section of the outline you may wish to write full sentences as headings, and they may become your topic sentences.

7. Begin to write. For many professionals as well as students, this is the most difficult part of writing, and we all have too many ways to put it off (taking more notes, watching the movie again, sharpening a pencil one more time). Delays do not make the task any easier. Making an outline can help because it consists of writing, but when it does not help enough, you should write down your ideas freely or randomly. Step back and imagine explaining your argument to a friend. Aim merely to get some sentences on paper; you can resort and refine your ideas later.

8. As you write, keep thinking about your subject, pushing your ideas farther, filling in gaps in your argument. Most of us don't know exactly what we think about a complex subject until we articulate our thoughts. Writing itself becomes a discovery process that we should take full advantage of. Check your logic by sketching an outline of what you have written. Polish your first paragraph and conclusion. Consider some larger questions about your approach: Is it mainly historical or formalistic? Are you interested in the cultural identity of the film? When you are emphasizing a particular method, decide to what extent this should be acknowledged early in your paper.

9. Revise, always revise. Allow as much time as possible between your first draft and your revision of it, preferably a few days. No one writes a perfect draft the first time, and most writers go

through several drafts before they feel comfortable and secure with an essay. If you grow weary, remind yourself: film scripts may be subjected to a dozen rewrites before a director starts to film, and once the film is made, the editing of it can become another series of revisions. The time you allow between your first draft and your revision should permit you to look at your essay with fresh eyes. Check logic, topic sentences, and the thesis statement (does it still fit the paper you wrote?). Check to see that you argue and develop your thesis rather than merely assert it. Read the essay through, watching for awkward expressions, poor transitions between sentences and paragraphs, and imprecise words. Are your examples still relevant? Are your quotations accurate? If you have time, put the paper aside again and do one last revision. Note: *If you type your essay on a word processor, it is very important that you revise at least one draft on a hard copy that has been printed out, since errors are easier to spot when the writing is in hard copy.*

10. Type, print out, or write a clean copy, following the guidelines on margins, footnotes, and so on (pp. 152–169). Be certain you are not breaking or bending the rules about plagiarism (pp. 157–160).

11. Proofread your final copy and insert necessary corrections (pp. 154-155).

6

Researching the Movies

Research improves any piece of writing. Normally, few people will see a film or begin an essay about it with all the facts or a record of other opinions before them. When you exchange opinions with a friend, exhaustive background information may not be necessary or even relevant. But as soon as you have a point to make or an argument to present, as soon as you have a stake in what you are saying, the more you know about the subject and the areas related to it, the more satisfying it will be to write about it.

Two equally intelligent friends may watch Paul Schrader's *Mishima* (1985), and although each may have sensitive and sensible responses to it, the one who has knowledge of Japanese culture or the facts of Mishima's life will have a richer and more detailed reading of the movie, and will be able to support an evaluation better. Although both may understand the themes and recognize how the elaborate structure and style are central ingredients in their reaction to them, the viewer who can connect those themes to other Schrader films, such as *Taxi Driver* (1976) or *Light Sleeper* (1992), will be able to detect variations and complexities in motifs of obsessiveness and alienation that escape the less knowledgeable viewer. If that person also takes the time to read Schrader's book *Transcendental Style,* some of Mishima's literary work, and something about Schrader's problems with the widow of the celebrated Japanese writer, that person could offer information and insights about the movie that would distinguish it from "just another opinion." A well-researched argument, one that brings to bear facts and observations outside the ken of the average viewer, is often all that distinguishes the authority and sophistication of one perspective from the impressions of another.

You can use research in a number of ways. It can be integrated into your essay to support your points with the authority of other writers. It can be used to introduce a common perception that you wish to argue against. Notice how this writer skillfully integrates background research on reactions to *Bad Timing* (1980) as a way of beginning her discussion:

> Nicholas Roeg's *Bad Timing: A Sensual Obsession* seems to have caused more displeasure than pleasure to virtually everyone: general audiences (it was not a box office success) and official media critics, on the one hand, and women's groups involved in the antipornography campaign, on the other. It has been found boring and confusing, over-reaching and pretentious, "technically good" and offensive to women. The X-rating and pattern of exhibition (art cinemas in first run, then, immediately, the revival circuit), plus the director's cult reputation (*Performance, Don't Look Now, Walkabout, The Man Who Fell to Earth*) place *Bad Timing* in a special category of commercially distributed, non-mainstream films . . . . (De Lauretis 87)

Most of us will have trouble including so much information in a short introduction, and sometimes a single provocative quotation can be enough to position your own point of view. Yet, however and wherever you use research, it can quickly substantiate and direct your writing if you use it wisely.

Writers of film essays are traditionally divided into two camps, distinguished by their approaches to research; one group is made up of critics and reviewers, the other of scholars and historians. Those in the first camp interpret a film through their own analysis and feelings about the value of the movie, and researching material other than what is on the screen is usually considered unnecessary. The scholar-historians, however, are concerned mostly with that other material, the history of the movie's production, critical responses to it, theoretical suppositions, and facts or information that are not at hand when you go to the movies. For the scholar-historian, understanding a movie involves a significant amount of research into the ideas and historical background that determine what appears on the screen. For the critic or reviewer, Orson Welles's *The Magnificent Ambersons* (1942) should speak for itself; the power of the story and the style of the movie would be the focus of discussion. For the historian, Welles's battles with the studio and his inability to complete the editing on his own terms become the most important part of the analysis.

Some writers emphasize either scholarship or a personal critical response, but most writers operate somewhere in between. Competent reviewers for a newspaper or a magazine usually bring a fair amount of knowledge (of film history, a director, the background of a particular film) to bear on their discussion of a movie. Likewise, good scholar-historians do not just accumulate "dry facts" or contemplate theoretical issues that have little to do with why we like or dislike a film. Their investigations will be based on a desire to throw more light on what certain movies mean or why we value them.

Research can involve anything from checking a date to examining the economic history of a film. Whether your topic is an interpretation of an individual movie or a description of the technology behind it, good research shapes a writer's feelings about how film can be understood and enjoyed. The writer of the following paragraph discusses a group of movies in the context of painstaking historical research into the development of camera movements; this research guides his evaluation of Marcel L'Herbier's *L'Argent* (1928).

Although it was not uncommon to find 10 or more tracking shots, not to mention large amounts of panning, during the length of some of the last American silent films such as *The Red Dance* (Raoul Walsh, 1928), in Europe this trend went a little further, particularly in France. In part this was because there were none of the constraints of early sound filming there until 1930, and in part because stylistic developments have always been pushed to greater lengths in the "Art Cinema" section of film production. So one gets some films like Marcel l'Herbier's *L'Argent* (1928) in which most of the shots involve camera movement of one kind or another, often of a very conspicuous nature. It seems likely to me that the obviousness of a lot of the camera movement in this film and others such as Jean Renoir's *Tire au Flanc* (1928) was due to lack of technical skill. This deduction follows from the fact that as *L'Argent* goes along the camera movement, though remaining just as extensive, becomes less conspicuous because it is fitted in better with the movements of the characters, presumably as a result of the practice that the director and operators acquired in the earlier part of the film. There have been a number of examples before and since of European film-makers learning their craft in front of the paying public. Something of the same lack of complete control can be seen in American films using a lot of camera movement at this date, but it does not go so far. (Salt 228)

HOW TO BEGIN RESEARCH

How much and what kind of research a writer does will depend on such variables as the time available and the length of the project. Having three months to write a twenty-page paper will presume and require more research than a five-page essay due in two weeks. A review written in two days will normally contain only the research that the writer has immediately available or that can be found in press notes; a scholarly essay will involve research done over many months.

The quality and amount of research material available depends on the film and when it was released. The writer who begins work on a classic film such as Victor Fleming's *Gone With the Wind* or Marcel Carné's *Children of Paradise (1945)* will find more essays and books than can be satisfactorily examined in a reasonable time. Conversely, in the months immediately after its release, even a highly publicized Hollywood film, such as *Hoffa* (1992) or *Malcolm X* (1992) will usually have generated only newspaper and magazine reviews and interviews. And a writer choosing to write on a recent foreign movie or an unheralded third-world film might have trouble locating even one or two short reviews. The usefulness of these materials can also be extremely different: a dozen superficial reviews of a film or a coffee-table book on a director may offer little more than variations on plot summaries or gossip, while a small, intelligent review or one exceptional book may provide you with an effective foundation or backdrop for your own ideas. Research is a learned skill, and the good writer develops methods of quickly finding what is available and efficiently sorting out what is most pertinent to his or her essay.

Each person develops an individual research technique. Some prefer to read background material before seeing a movie. Some work better when they think through their position on a film and then investigate how that position contrasts with or compliments the existing body of opinion. Many writers' habits fall somewhere between these extremes.

Even before seeing a movie, try to get a sense of it by considering preliminary questions about it (when it was made, its intended audience; see Chapter 2). After seeing the movie, clarify your thoughts about it and what interests you most. (Writing about something you find uninteresting can be the most difficult kind of writing.) Once you have sketched your ideas about a movie and focused those ideas on one or two topics, you have parameters within which to direct your research. This kind of preliminary focus can be particularly important when your topic has generated a great deal of critical literature through the years, since it allows you to distinguish what is relevant to your argument and what is not. The student who intends to write on a Godard film, for instance, can easily be intimidated by the large number of books and critical essays on him. When the student focuses his or her research on "the use of sound in the recent work of Godard," the task immediately becomes more manageable. Keep in mind that, although some subjects can prove too large for a paper, very few will be too small if you think carefully about them. The most important guide is your own interest.

Research should be done with an open and discriminating mind. A good writer is willing to be redirected down new paths and, if necessary, to change a position. The student researching Godard and sound may, upon reading other writers, decide to work instead on the spoken dialogue or to do more research into Godard's video experiments to learn how they affected the sound in his later films. The writer disappointed with the comparatively little serious work on a period in film history (such as that of Nazi Germany) must be ready to explore topics outside film history by reading more general cultural or political histories. Research both develops and tests your ideas. Adjusting or changing ideas is part of the excitement of doing research.

The trick is to learn to recognize what is important to your essay and what is not, what to keep and what to discard. The process is made easier when you are at the same time prepared with ideas and flexible about changing them. René Clair's description of filmmaking suggests a similar process for researching and writing about film: "The idea for a film is sometimes born in an author's mind, but more often a film company has the intention of making a film and is thus moved to search among existing ideas for the one that suits it best."

When you have researched a subject and reworked your original idea, it is advisable to see a movie again. With a sharpened sense of what you want to say, you will invariably discover new information and find previously missed images that support your ideas. Just as your research is influenced by your first ideas after seeing the movie, your sense of what you want to say is sharpened by seeing the film again. The inverse of Godard's pronouncement is thus "said better, seen better."

THE MATERIALS OF RESEARCH

Research materials are conventionally divided into primary sources and secondary sources. Primary sources are the films themselves and material directly involved in the films. Secondary sources are the books, essays, and reviews you read about the movie. A person planning to write on the movies of George Roy Hill would go first to the primary sources: the movies themselves, a recording of the sound track, and even the script if available. After consulting the primary sources, the writer may investigate such secondary sources as a review, a film history, and a book on Hill.

Primary Sources

With film research, even gaining access to a primary source can pose some difficulties. Researching a movie has always been inhibited by the real obstacle of not being able to see the movie when you want and as often as you would like. If your subject is a mainstream movie that happens to be playing at a local theater, this difficulty is relieved somewhat, since you will be able to see the movie several times, or as long as your financial resources hold out. Frequently, though, the films that interest you are not in regular distribution, and special strategies are required to supplement a first screening.

VIDEO

A seasoned researcher often uses archives or special arrangements with distributors to view authoritative versions of movies that have been damaged or cut though the years. Students, who usually have neither access to nor need of these facilities, must discover easier ways to view the films they are studying. Today videotapes, discs, and movies on cable networks substitute for or supplement the films themselves. But this form of film must be viewed with caution and skepticism for several reasons: the quality of the image is usually inferior, the original color or black and white tends to "wash out" (or a black-and-white film may be "colorized"), the frame format and focus can be reduced or altered in ways that change significantly the meaning of the images, and images or sequences may have been edited out completely. Many films, from *The Ten Commandments* (1956) to *E.T.* (1982), rely on the wide-screen image, and, even with the use of letter-box formats for television screens, the video-screen image is dramatically different from the original. Finally, home viewing conditions create a very different kind of response to a movie than a theatrical screening does. Viewers might have very different experiences of Griffith's *Intolerance* (1916) or Kubrick's *2001: A Space Odyssey* if they watch one of these films on a movie screen and then on a video monitor.

Videotapes, laser discs, and cable movies are here to stay, and it would be a mistake to deny their value for film research. With more and more films aimed at television showings, and with an increasing number of television directors moving awkwardly into film, the aesthetic and commercial line between the two media is becoming less distinct. In fact, some movies we see at a theater these days seem to have been made for the television screen. More important, the widespread availability of video recorders and the resurrection of foreign and forgotten films on tape, disc, or cable make these tools an almost indispensable aid to film research. A writer should make every attempt to see a film first on a movie screen, but the advantage of being able to further analyze that movie on tape or disc is considerable. A student can study a single sequence or even a single frame in detail; other films by a director or from the same period can be compared, and more esoteric movies are becoming available at video stores than are available through film distributors.

SCRIPTS

Published scripts are a primary source for studying a film. Unfortunately, few scripts are available beyond a selection of "classic" movies, and the kind of information they offer varies a great deal. A writer researching a film whose script has been published may find in it merely dialogue. Sometimes he or she may also find camera directions and detailed shot reproductions. One recent series of this kind, from Rutgers University Press, contains interviews and essays about each movie. Keep in mind that published screenplays of films can differ significantly from the "shooting script" and from the film itself; never base an analysis totally on a published screenplay.

Secondary Sources: Books, Indexes, and Journals

Film books abound, and you should begin your research into secondary sources by checking the card catalogue in your library for what is available on your subject. Look under "Movies," "Film," "Cinema," and "Motion Pictures," as well as under headings that deal specifically with your subject matter. If your topic concerns horror movies of the thirties, for example, check for relevant titles under the four main headings, then look for titles under "Horror Films" or "The Supernatural." You could also check the headings for national cinemas that relate to your subject (e.g., "German Cinema"). While researching these titles in card catalogues, it is efficient and practical to write down bibliographical information — author, full title, publisher, and publication place and date — on note cards, even if you do not use all those references.

In addition to the card catalogues, students researching a topic are encouraged to take advantage of the growing number of electronic database systems. Many of the widely available systems, such as *Academic Index, Nexis/Lexis,* and *Comindex,* incorporate research on film and cinema studies. More traditional research sources such as the *MLA International Bibliography* or *Magill's Survey of Cinema* can also be found on electronic databases. Your research librarian can tell you which database systems available in your library contain material pertinent to your work. Accessing these systems from a single computer screen is often an extremely efficient means of doing research.

Once you have gathered the appropriate books, there follows the task of culling the information you need from a sometimes large pile. One way to start is to scan the preface or jacket cover to learn whether a book deals with the material in a useful way. The table of contents will tell you if the chapter titles point in the direction of your own thinking. When your topic concerns one or more specific movies, consult the index of the book to see how frequently and fully those films are discussed. Some books on horror films may be irrelevant "picture books"; others may be detailed histories that become helpful only after you have a better understanding of your topic. To separate the books that offer either too little or too much information from those that seem to address your subject and films most appropriately, select one or two that seem most manageable to serve as your introductory texts. If they prove satisfactory and helpful, use their bibliographies to guide you toward other sources.

Besides the many specialized books on film that can be found in a library, there are guides, encyclopedias, and film dictionaries that provide quick access to dates and historical information about a movie, a director, or a film movement. Although these works rarely offer analysis or argument about a film, they give solid factual information and introductory commentaries. Of the many available, here is a sampling:

Aaronson, Charles S. *International Motion Picture and Television Almanac.* New York: Quigley Publications, 1930–. Annual.

Ash, Rene. *The Motion Picture Film Editor.* Metuchen, NJ: Scarecrow Press, 1974.

Bawden, Liz-Anne, ed. *The Oxford Companion to Film.* New York: Oxford University Press, 1976.

Bergan, Ronald and Robyn Karney. *The Faber Companion to Foreign Films.* London: Faber & Faber, 1992.

Cawkwell, Tim, and John M. Smith. *The World Encyclopedia of Film.* New York: A & W Visual Library, 1972.

Corliss, Richard, ed. *The Hollywood Screenwriters.* New York: Avon, 1972.

Corliss, Richard. *Talking Pictures: Screenwriters in the American Cinema.* New York: Overlook Press, 1974.

Cowie, Peter, ed. *International Film Guide.* New York: A. S. Barnes, 1964–. Annual.

Enser, A. G. S., ed. *Filmed Books and Plays: 1928–1974.* New York: Academic Press, 1974.

Film Daily Year Book of Motion Pictures. New York: Film Daily Publishers, 1918–.

Gottesman, Ronald, and Harry M. Geduld. *Guidebook to Film: An Eleven-in-One Reference.* New York: Holt, Rinehart & Winston, 1972.

Graham, Peter, ed. *Dictionary of the Cinema.* London: Tantivy Press, 1964.

Halliwell, Leslie; John Walker, ed. *Halliwell's Filmgoer's and Video Viewer's Companion.* 10th ed. New York: HarperCollins, 1993.

Halliwell, Leslie. *Halliwell's Film Guide.* 6th ed. New York: Scribners, 1987.

Higham, Charles. *Hollywood Cameramen.* Bloomington: Indiana University Press, 1970.

Kaplan, Mike, ed. *Variety International Showbusiness Reference.* New York: Garland, 1981.

Katz, Ephraim. *The Film Encyclopedia.* New York: Putnam, 1982.

Kozarski, Richard, ed. *Hollywood Directors, 1914-1940*. New York: Oxford University Press, 1976.

Kozarski, Richard, ed. *Hollywood Directors, 1941–1976*. New York: Oxford University Press, 1977.

Krafsur, Richard, ed. *The American Film Institute Catalogue of Motion Pictures Produced in the United States: Feature Films, 1961–1970*. New York: R. R. Bowker, 1976.

Magill's Survey of Cinema. Englewood Cliffs, NJ. Annual.

Maltin, Leonard, ed. *TV Movies*. Revised ed. New York: Signet Books, 1991.

Manchell, Frank. *Film Study: A Resource Guide*. Rutherford, NJ: Fairleigh Dickinson University Press, 1973.

Manvell, Roger, and Lewis Jacobs, eds. *International Encyclopedia of Film*. New York: Crown, 1972.

Mayer, Michael, ed. *The Film Industries*. New York: Hastings House, 1978.

Milne, Tom, ed. *The Time Out Film Guide*. London: Penguin, 1991.

Monaco, James. *Film: How and Where to Find Out What You Want to Know*. New York: Zoetrope, 1976.

Munden, Kenneth W., ed. *The American Film Institute Catalogue of Motion Pictures Produced in the United States: Feature Films 1921-1930*. 2 vols. New York: R. R. Bowker, 1971.

The New York Times Directory of the Film. New York: Arno, 1974.

The New York Times Film Reviews, 1913-1970. 7 vols. New York: Arno, 1971.

Pirie, David, ed. *Anatomy of the Movies*. New York: Macmillan, 1981.

Rehrauer, George. *The Macmillan Film Bibliography*. 2 vols. London and New York: Macmillan, 1982.

Roud, Richard, ed. *A Critical Dictionary of the Cinema*. New York: Viking, 1980.

Sadoul, Georges. *Dictionary of Film Makers*. Trans. and ed. by Peter Morris. Berkeley: University of California Press, 1972.

Sadoul, Georges. *Dictionary of Films*. Trans. and ed. by Peter Morris. Berkeley: University of California Press, 1972.

Sarris, Andrew. *The American Cinema: Directors and Directions, 1929-1968*. New York: Dutton, 1968.

Sitney, P. Adams. *The American Avant-Garde*. New York: Oxford University Press, 1974.

Speed, F. Maurice. *Film Review*. London: W. H. Allen, 1966–. Annual.

Spottiswoode, Raymond, et al. *The Focal Encyclopedia of Film & Television Techniques*. New York: Hastings House, 1969.

Steinberg, Corbett. *Reel Facts: The Movie Book of Records*. Updated ed. New York: Vintage, 1981.

Thomson, David. *A Biographical Dictionary of Film*. New York: Morrow, 1976.

Variety Movie Guide. Englewood Cliffs, NJ: Prentice-Hall, 1992.

Willis, John, ed. John Willis' *Screen World*. New York: Crown, 1949-. Annual.

The most important and up-to-date sources for film research, along with scholarly books, are journals and magazines. A writer gradually becomes familiar with the differences among them, learning to judge which ones will be most helpful for which topics. The essays and reviews found here can provide a range of information: interviews with actors, scriptwriters, and directors, background facts on the production of the movie, investigations of complex critical issues (the politics or the formal features of the movie, for instance). A first step in researching articles on a specific movie or topic is to scan a good index. This should list the majority of essays and reviews on your subject and indicate the periodicals in which they are found. But keep in mind that the titles or information you seek may be located only under such general headings as "Motion Pictures" or "Movies." Besides more general indexes such as the *Guide to Periodical Literature* and the film section of the *MLA International Bibliography,* the following are the standard indexes for film research:

Aceto, Vincent J., Jane Graves, and Fred Silva. *Film Literature Index*. Albany, NY: Filmdex Inc. Quarterly.

Batty, Linda. *Retrospective Index to Film Periodicals 1930-1971*. New York: R. R. Bowker, 1975.

Bowles, Stephen E., ed. *Index to Critical Film Reviews in British and American Periodicals 1930-1972*. New York: Burt Franklin, 1973.

Bowles, Stephen E., ed. *Index to Critical Reviews of Books About Film, 1930-1972*. New York: Burt Franklin, 1975.

Bukalski, Peter J. *Film Research: A Critical Bibliography with Annotation and Essay*. Boston: G. K. Hall, 1972.

Gerlach, John C., and Lana Gerlach. *The Critical Index*. New York: Teacher's College Press, 1974.

International Index to Film Periodicals (FIAF Index). New York: R. R. Bowker, 1972–. Annual.

Kowalski, Rosemary Ribich. *Women and Film: A Bibliography*. Metuchen, NJ: Scarecrow Press, 1976.

Media Review Digest. Ann Arbor, MI: Pierian Press, 1970-.

MacCann, Richard Dyer, and Edward S. Perry. *The New Film Index: A Bibliography of Magazine Articles in English, 1930-1970*. New York: Dutton, 1974.

Monaco, James, and Susan Schenker, eds. *Books About Film: A Bibliographical Checklist*. 3rd ed. New York: Zoetrope, 1976.

Schuster, Mel. *Motion Picture Directors: A Bibliography of Magazine and Periodical Articles, 1900-1969*. Metuchen, NJ: Scarecrow Press, 1973.

When consulting these indexes, it is best to begin with more recent years and move back through earlier years to find relevant essays; the more current articles often have more up-to-date information. Noting the entries over a period of several years is usually a good start. A just-released movie, however, may not appear in the most current index, and in this case, you must examine the tables of contents of the most recent journals and the movie reviews in newspapers that have appeared in the last few months. Caution: invariably an index will use extreme abbreviations for the journals; be certain to check the key to those abbreviations before leaving the index.

Film journals vary considerably in quality and focus, and the following list of titles indicates the variety and range of journals that a film researcher might encounter. Some publications offer difficult theoretical essays; others have mainly interviews and short review articles; still others (like *Variety)* are a regular source of trade and industry information. Although those marked with an asterix feature articles particularly useful for college students, you should investigate all that seem to deal with your topic. By using them, you will become familiar with their advantages and limitations. In addition to these more specialized periodicals, most magazines and newspapers (such as *Newsweek* and *The New York Times)* are regular sources for movie reviews and short, general articles.

> *American Cinematographer* (monthly). Short essays, industry information
>
> *American Film* (ten per year). Review articles, short essays
>
> *Cahiers du Cinéma* (monthly, in French). Theoretical essays, current film reviews, occasional interviews
>
> *Camera Obscura* (irregularly). Theoretical and feminist essays on film, television, popular culture
>
> *Cinema Journal* (quarterly). Critical essays
>
> *Cinema Nuovo* (bimonthly, in Italian). Critical essays and current film reviews
>
> *Cineaste* (quarterly). Critical essays (usually directed at ideological issues), interviews, current film reviews
>
> *Filmfacts* (bimonthly). Short reviews of current films
>
> *Film Comment* (bimonthly). Critical essays
>
> *Film Criticism* (three per year). Critical essays
>
> *Film Quarterly* (quarterly). Critical essays, occasional interviews, current film reviews
>
> *Film Reader* (yearly). Critical essays
>
> *Film und Fernsehen* (monthly, in German). Critical essays, interviews, feminist emphasis
>
> *Films and Filming* (monthly). Short articles, current film reviews
>
> *Films in Review* (monthly). Short reviews
>
> *Focus on Films* (quarterly). Short reviews
>
> *Framework* (irregularly). Theoretical and critical essays.
>
> *Frauen und Film* (quarterly, in German)

⋆*Iris* (irregularly, in French and English). Critical and theoretical essays

Jeune Cinéma (nine per year, in French). Critical essays, interviews, current film reviews

⋆*Journal of Film and Video* (quarterly). Critical essays on film, television, video

⋆*Jump Cut* (bimonthly). Critical essays directed often at political and ideological issues, current film reviews, some interviews

Journal of Popular Film and Television (quarterly)

Kino: German Film (quarterly). Short articles and essays on the contemporary German film industry.

⋆*Literature/Film Quarterly* (quarterly). Critical essays on topics related to the intersections of film and literature

⋆*Millennium* (irregularly). Theoretical and critical essays

Millimeter (monthly). Short articles and essays

Monthly Film Bulletin (monthly). Critical essays

Movietone News (irregularly). Short articles and critical essays

⋆*Positif* (monthly, in French). Critical and theoretical essays

⋆*Persistence of Vision* (irregularly). Critical and theoretical essays

⋆*Quarterly Review of Film and Television Studies* (quarterly). Critical essays on film and television

⋆*Screen* (quarterly). Theoretical essays

⋆*Sight and Sound* (monthly). Critical essays and current film reviews

⋆*Velvet Light Trap* (quarterly). Critical essays

Variety (weekly). Short articles with current film industry and commercial information

⋆*Wide Angle* (quarterly). Critical and theoretical essays

TAKING NOTES ON SECONDARY SOURCES

Taking notes on secondary sources requires judgment. If you have an idea or a topic firmly in mind as you begin to read, you will need to decide what supports, challenges, or complicates that idea. If you are still trying to clarify your own argument, you will need to read with an open but discriminating mind that allows you to be guided by other opinions while being critical of opinions you do not agree with. Often, reading a good essay on a film can provide the one sentence or paragraph that crystalizes your own idea about the movie and points you along your own path. Be open to suggestions, and be willing to follow leads, whether they are ideas or other sources.

When possible, skim or read quickly the essay or chapter to get a general idea. Then, if it seems noteworthy, reread it and begin taking notes immediately (many writers use four-by-six-inch cards and may write on one or both sides of the card). It can help to number the cards that relate to a single source, or to place a subject heading at the top of each card to help you sort them according to the logic of your paper. Once you have a sense of an article or a chapter, use these guidelines in transferring material to notecards:

1. Either summarize ideas from a section of your source or quote exactly those sentences or passages that may prove useful. If you use an exact quotation, place it in quotation marks. Whether you summarize or quote, be certain to indicate all the necessary information about the source, including page numbers.

2. When quoting sentences or passages directly, be discriminating. Do not simply copy long paragraphs that seem important but that you have not entirely digested or understood. If you consider carefully those passages that may be helpful to your argument later, the research will help refine your argument at an early stage. No one incorporates every note or summary gathered from secondary sources into the final draft. But if you use judgment and reflect on the material you are choosing, you will not be faced with a massive pile of notecards that have scattered rather than clarified your ideas.

3. Never change occasional words in a quoted passage and copy it as if it were a summary. If the passage later appears in your essay, it will look very much like plagiarism.

4. Sometimes it is advantageous to omit words or phrases from a quotation, because they are not relevent to your point. When you do this, indicate the omission with an ellipsis (three spaced periods).

5. Whether you are summarizing or quoting directly, you may wish to jot down your own response to the material, such as "Galperin is the only critic to recognize how literary this movie is." Be sure to mark off clearly these reflections from the quoted or summarized passage, either with brackets or double parentheses.

WRITING THE PAPER

Once you have done your preliminary research, you will move toward a polished essay by integrating that research into a finished draft of your argument. Normally, research papers can be anywhere from 2000 to 6000 words long (eight to twenty-four double-spaced, typed pages), and the writer should always make the amount and kind of research fit the length of the essay. Here are guidelines:

1. Begin by rereading the notes you have taken and sorting them into categories, for example, "historical background material" and "themes." Not all the information you have gathered will necessarily be useful as you focus your topic. A good writer learns to differentiate between what is truly useful and what is not. Overloading your essay with an enormous number of quotations will not improve it; needless information will only bury your argument. If you have sketched an outline, this is the time to rework it in light of your research. This reworking of the outline may involve only fine tuning: adding transition sections, expanding a section. Or you may find you have to rethink your most important premise, shifting and restructuring it to account for recent findings. If your original approach was based on auteurist presumptions that are out of line with the limited control the director had over the particular film, the facts will require you to reformulate your argument. As you develop this draft, you should be able to state a fairly clear and precise thesis for the paper.

2. Leave plenty of room between the lines and in the margins to add and rearrange information. Some research might work better in an earlier section; another sentence may be needed to

get from point A to point B. Allow yourself the freedom to adjust your material as you adjust and rework your argument.

3. Write or type your quotations exactly as they will appear in your final draft. Put short quotations (under five lines) between quotation marks and run them into your text. Longer quotations are not enclosed within quotation marks but instead are indented and separated from your prose by a triple space. *Be certain to check that you have copied the quotations accurately*.

4. Add to your quotations all relevant bibliographical information. This material will appear later in your list of works cited, but you will find it advantageous to have it before you, to easily identify the source, when you do your final draft .

5. Get all titles, dates, and technical information right at this point. Include the date a film was released in parentheses following the title. If you intend to use both the foreign language title and the English release title, this is when you should doublecheck both. When using an author's name in your text, use the full name as it appears on the article, book, or review. In subsequent references to this author, use just the last name (it is unnecessary in most cases to use a title like "Professor" or "Ms").

6. This early draft may be the best time to write out concrete descriptions of shots or sequences you refer to. When your points require reference to other films as examples, consider and insert those titles.

7. When you revise this draft, introduce your research and quotations so that you get the most out of them. Cramming all your research into one section or introducing each quotation with "A says . . . . B says" (or worse yet, no introductory phrase at all) suggests that you have not considered carefully how best to use your research. A good rhetorical strategy is to suggest how you feel about the material by remarking "In this perceptive review of the film" or "A typical but superficial response to the movie is summed up in this comment." Short remarks or phrases can be integrated directly into your prose and simply annotated:

```
The closing is, as one writer put it, "a confus-
ing assault on the viewer" (King 121).
```

If you are contrasting interpretations, make that clear in the way you use and introduce quotations or paraphrases. In the end, your readers should feel that they have not only heard a specific and well-formulated argument, but that it has been based on sound judgments about the film, the facts surrounding the film, and the perceptions of other knowledgeable viewers.

8. If you make your final draft easy to read, it will be much easier to type.

9. After you have typed or printed out a final draft of the essay, check the titles, dates, and page numbers of all your biblio graphical information. Be sure you have included all works used in the "Works Cited" section (pp. 163–166) and, if you choose, all works that you consulted (but perhaps did not use) in a "Works Consulted" section (p. 163).

10. Always make a copy of the paper before submitting it in case the original is lost or misplaced by you or your instructor.

SAMPLE ESSAYS

The following are two versions of the same essay: one relies on an intelligent writer's careful reflection on the movie; the other develops that knowledge through a moderate amount of research. Both versions are competent, but the second carries a rhetorical force and an authority that distinguish it. Notice also how research can do more than just support your original ideas: it can help the writer to develop those ideas further and even change their direction.

Katherine Smith

Images of Violence in Penn's Bonnie and Clyde

Arthur Penn's Bonnie and Clyde is basically a
gangster movie which glorifies the lives of Bonnie
Parker and Clyde Barrow, two young criminals on the run
in the thirties. Thematically, one of the most striking
features of the film is how these small-time hoodlums

become larger-than-life heroes in a society which seems to be crumbling in every way. Stylistically, the film is also remarkable. Through a number of stunning shots, which culminate in the grotesque killing of the pair at the conclusion of the film, the movie seems constantly to call attention to itself as a movie about image-making. Integrating these themes and style in a gripping and suspenseful story, Bonnie and Clyde is an unusual and perplexing movie about the bizarre relationship between two people's desperate need to escape the daily miseries of their society and the violence that is necessary for that escape.

One of the unusual variations in this gangster film is that the heroes (or anti-heroes) are also victims, clownish drifters who become involved in a life of crime mainly because they need an identity of one sort or another. These public enemies never seem to demonstrate any of the real malice or the professional confidence that is associated with a gangster of the James Cagney variety. Through the work of carefully framed and emptied shots, the land they live in seems a wasteland, the people they encounter mostly sad and poor. Bonnie joins Clyde in her first robbery attempt because she is bored, lonely, and looking for some excitement, and, in a later scene, Clyde seems shocked and confused that one of his victims should actually defend himself by trying to kill Clyde.

More importantly, as the film progresses, these two gangsters seem motivated more by the wish to see their names and pictures in the paper than a wish to accumulate large amounts of money (which is rarely discussed by the gang). When Clyde's brother, Buck, comes to visit, Bonnie and Clyde have their pictures taken in the theatrical pose of gangsters, and for them, this kind of exaggerated image of themselves—mostly in the paper and the public's imagination—is what allows them to have a real identity in their depression-ravaged society. Summing up their true reason for their violent life of crime, Clyde convinces Bonnie to join him by exclaiming: "Everybody'd know about us!"

In this sense, these two criminals are not just victims of their society (an old cliché) but victims of the sensationalism which they need and which the press panders to. (This seems more true today than it possibly could have in the thirties.) In a way, their need for those glossy images of themselves is what seals their fate, since it is their humiliation of the Texas Ranger with a newspaper photo that motivates him to hunt them down. Ultimately, to put this succinctly, they are trapped in the logic of their desire for glorious self-images, just as Clyde toward the end of the film is—tragically and comically—unable to envision a different kind of life, but only different tactics for robbing banks.

The sensational climax and conclusion of the movie is consequently entirely appropriate. That the death of the two "heroes" follows a scene in which they read Bonnie's poetic description of their adventures and

then make love for the first time is a summary statement of the movie's logic. When Clyde reads the ballad
he says, "You've told our story . . . . you've made us
somebody." They have found, in short, the identities
and public images they have been searching for, and
they are now able to consummate their love. The slow-
motion, multi-angled death that follows can be seen,
moreover, as an extension of the newfound identities.
Trapped in the logic of sensationalism and public
images, they, in the end, find themselves only in the
sensational movie images in which they die.

Katherine Simith

Images of Violence in Penn's Bonnie and Clyde

Although Bonnie and Clyde still retains much of its
original power, it may be difficult for contemporary
audiences to appreciate fully the impact of this
extremely successful movie. In his History of Narrative
Film, David Cook summarizes the tumultuous reception of
this tumultuous movie:

> A new American cinema and a new American film
> audience announced themselves emphatically with
> the release in 1967 of Arthur Penn's Bonnie and
> Clyde. This film, which was universally attacked
> by the critics when it opened in August, had by
> November become the most popular film of the year.
> It would subsequently receive ten Academy Awards

nominations and win two . . . , win the New York
Film Critics' Award for Best Script . . . and be
named the Best Film of 1967 by many of the critics
who had originally panned it. Most triumphant of
all, perhaps, Bonnie and Clyde is the only film
ever to have forced the public retraction of a
critical opinion by Time magazine. . . . Indeed,
the phenomenal success of Bonnie and Clyde caused
many retractions on the part of veteran film
critics who, on first viewing, had mistaken it for
a conventional bloody, gangster film. (626)

There is, of course, no denying that the movie is
basically a bloody descendant of the gangster genre,
and it does present itself, through its documentary
style and the photos that are used during the credit
sequence, as a portrait of the thirties. But the
confused initial response to the movie indicates, I
believe, that there is something more going on: that
Penn, through the self-conscious style he supposedly
learned from the French New Wave,[1] is offering a
more complicated commentary on modern images of
violence in America and a disturbing critique of how
Americans have escaped into those images, especially
during the sixties.

---

[1] The influence of directors like Godard, Truffaut,
and Chabrol on Penn and other American directors is
often remarked in film histories. In general, these
new, confrontational styles began to make their appearance in the United States in the mid-sixties.

There are several signs that this is more than a gangster movie. Most notably, in this gangster film, the heroes (or anti-heroes) seem also victims, clownish drifters who become involved in a life of crime mainly because they need an identify of one sort or another. These public enemies never seem to demonstrate any of the real malice or the professional confidence associated with the James Cagney variety of gangster; likewise, the world they live in lacks all the glamour of a gangster's world. Through the work of carefully framed and emptied shots, the land they drive through seems a wasteland, the people they encounter mostly sad and poor. Bonnie joins Clyde in her first robbery attempt because she is bored, lonely, and looking for some excitement, and, in a later scene Clyde seems shocked and confused that one of his victims should actually defend himself by trying to kill Clyde.

More importantly, as the film progresses, these two gangsters seem motivated more by the wish to see their names and pictures in the paper than a wish to accumulate large amounts of money (which is rarely discussed by the gang). When Clyde's brother, Buck, comes to visit, Bonnie and Clyde have their pictures taken in the theatrical poses of gangsters, and, for them, these kinds of exaggerated images of themselves—mostly found in the papers and the public's imagination—are what allows them to have a real identity apart from their depression-ravaged society. Summing up their true reason for their violent life of crime, Clyde convinces

Bonnie to join him by exclaiming: "Everybody'd know about us!" These two criminals are not just victims of their society (an old cliché) but victims of the sensationalism which they need and which the press panders to.

This connection between violence and publicity seems to me to make Bonnie and Clyde as much about the late sixties as about the thirties. In the late sixties, when the violence of Vietnam was on everyone's television screen, the media was pandering to and creating sensational violence as never before.[2] As Pauline Kael has perceptively observed, although the "Vietnam war has barely been mentioned on the screen, . . . you can feel it in Bonnie and Clyde" (225). Where specifically an audience can most see and feel that war is, I believe, not only in the large amounts of graphic violence in the film but, more significantly, in the way the movie logically links its violence to the sensationalism of the media coverage. In a way, Bonnie and Clyde's need for glossy images of themselves is what motivates them and what seals their fate, since it is their humiliation of the Texas Ranger with a newspaper photo that results in his relentlessly hunting them down. They are trapped in the violent logic of their

---

[2]The ambiguous but unprecedented role of the public media in the Vietnam War is probably best summed up by the common observation that it was "the first war fought on television."

desire for glorious self-images—just as Clyde toward the end of the movie is (tragically and comically) unable to envision a different kind of life but only different tactics for robbing banks. Bonnie and Clyde, in short, are neither simply thirties gangsters surviving through crime, nor sixties rebels searching for identities. They are mindless victims of a glorious and violent sensationalism, the same sensationalism with which a public media created a confused national identity during the war-torn sixties.

The sensational climax and conclusion is consequently entirely appropriate in a film about the search for identity in a violent society. That the death of the two "heroes" follows scenes in which they read Bonnie's poetic description of their adventure in the newspaper and then make love for the first time is a summary statement of the film's logic. When Clyde reads the ballad, he says, "You've told our story. . . . you've made us somebody." They have found, in short, the identities and public images they have been searching for, and they are now able to consummate their love. The slow-motion, multi-angled death that follows can be seen, moreover, as an extension of that newfound identity. Trapped in the logic of violent sensationalism and public images, they aptly find themselves only in the violent and sensational movie images in which they die.

As an indirect image of the sixties, Bonnie and

Clyde may not be, however, as much a statement of despair as it seems. If Bonnie and Clyde are trapped, Penn's movie may work to untrap its 1967 audience through its self-conscious and graphic assault on them. Like the French New Wave directors, Penn may be attempting to make his audience consider more actively the violent images through which they live. In that sense, the confused and contradictory response to Bonnie and Clyde may be an indication that it achieved its aim.

Works Cited

Cook, David. A History of Narrative Film. New York:
    Norton, 1981
Kael, Pauline, Reeling. New York: Warner Books, 1972.

7
Manuscript Form

MANUSCRIPT COPY

Although every instructor has individual expectations and requirements about the final form in which an essay should be submitted, there are general guidelines that all writers follow when putting an essay into its final form.

1. Type the paper. Although typing an essay may be difficult for some students and although some instructors may not require it, typed copy does make a difference. A cleanly typed manuscript simply looks more professional and is easier to read. A typed paper gives you an edge with your reader, who will see your work from the beginning as something you took seriously. Some writers find that a typed copy allows them to read and revise their work from a new perspective. When you have the time and the typing (or word-processing) skills, it can be a real advantage to revise a typed draft.

2. Use clean, 8½-by-11-inch paper, typed on one side, with a fresh ribbon that produces sharp, easily readable type. When you use a word processor, the edges of the computer paper should be as clean as possible, stripped of perforations.

3. Most instructors prefer that you put your name, date, and course number on three lines in the corner of the first page. Separate title pages are normally unnecessary, and fancy accessories (a folder cover or a clear plastic binder) merely waste money and add bulk to the instructor's load of essays.

4. It is not necessary to number the first page, but be certain to

number all following pages. Usually page numbers appear at the top of each page, in the center or the right-hand corner. Numbers centered at the bottom of the page are also acceptable.

5. Leave uniform and adequate margins on each page: an inch or an inch and a half on both sides and at the top and the bottom of the page. It is silly to think that larger margins will somehow disguise a short paper.

6. Double-space all copy, except for long quotes, which are indented and single-spaced. (The MLA guide says double-space even the long, indented passages, but this practice is mainly used for essays being submitted to journals for publication.)

7. Center your title two inches (twelve lines) from the top of the first page in order to identify clearly the title and the beginning of the essay. Begin your essay one inch below the title. Capitalize the first letter of each word in your title, except prepositions, articles, and conjunctions. Underline only the titles of films that appear in your title. Do not underline or use quotation marks around any other part of your title, unless that part comes from another source and requires punctuation marks. Thus a standard title would appear like this:

Conrad, Coppola, and <u>Apocalypse Now</u>

When you use a quotation from another source within your title, the quoted material appears in quotation marks:

Versions of a <u>Heart of Darkness</u>:

"The Horror, the Horror" of <u>Apocalypse Now</u>

When a title does not fit easily on one line, a second line is preferable to crowding a title within the width of a page. The second line should also be centered.

8. Indent each new paragraph five spaces from the left margin.

9. Most instructors do not expect stills to accompany your essay, nor is it an especially good idea to include a showy still that serves only to dress up your paper. However, when an essay is focused on a single shot or a series of shots, it can be extremely helpful to reproduce a still or series of stills in an appendix at the end of the paper. If you can obtain a pertinent still or stills, be

sure that it is reproduced and labeled clearly, that you identify its place in the film when you discuss it in your text, and that you refer explicitly to the reproduction at that point: "In *Apocalypse Now,* the insane theatrics of politics crystalize in the Playboy Bunny Show deep in the jungle (see Appendix 1)."

10. Always make a copy of your essay to keep in case your original is lost or misplaced.

11. Staple your paper in the upper left-hand corner.

LAST-MINUTE CORRECTIONS

Writers are prone to last-minute revisions or corrections. After your paper is in its final, typed form, corrections should be kept to a minimum, since too many pencilled-in changes can spoil the effect of a cleanly typed manuscript. As you proofread your typed copy, however, you will discover small errors, misspellings, and typographical mistakes, that can be corrected neatly by using proofreading symbols and markings.

When one or two words are incorrect, they can easily be changed by crossing out the wrong words or letters and printing the necessary corrections above it:

Before 1917, Russian film culture ~~were~~ ^WAS^ mainly European.

To add a word or a phrase, use a caret in the appropriate space:

Before 1917, Russian ^film^ culture was mainly European.

Transpositions of letters or words are done in this way:

Before 1917, Russian film culture mainly⟋was European.

To separate words that have been run together, insert a vertical line; close unnecessary gaps with a curved line connecting the letters to be joined:

Before 1917, Russian fil⌣m culture was|mainly European.

A final proofreading may reveal that a paragraph should be divided or broken into two. Use the paragraph symbol to indicate where a new paragraph should start:

> Many do not even consider Russian movies before revolu-
> tionary figures like Vertov and Eisenstein. ¶ Before
> 1917, Russian film culture was mainly European.

QUOTATIONS

In writing about film, you will have to deal with two kinds of quotations:

1. In quoting dialogue or commentary from the film itself, normally no footnotes are necessary, and the words quoted can be integrated directly into your text.
2. In quoting from essays, books, or interviews with individuals involved with the production, you will need some kind of footnote and documentation. When the quotations are short passages (less than five lines), they can be inserted directly into your prose:

> One prominent critic has described this film as "a
> study in postmodern emptiness."

Whether a paper is short or long has little to do with the use of quotations, but when quotations are used they should be punctuated properly and spread judiciously throughout the essay (never make an essay a string of quotations). The following are general guidelines:

1. Whatever you are quoting, be accurate, and check the quoted passages when you proofread. In most cases, quotations should correspond exactly to the original in spelling, capitalization, and punctuation. When you add material within the quotation, put those words in brackets. When you underline a word or phrase to emphasize it, note that it is your emphasis in parentheses after the quotation:

> Many factors distinguished the American studios

```
of the thirties, but, in the words of one historian,
"the hierarchy of American studios [in the thirties]
was in some crucial ways determined by the class of
audience they targeted" (my emphasis).
```

If you omit unnecessary words within a quoted passage, signal the omission with three spaced periods, called an ellipsis:

```
In the words of one historian, "the hierarchy of
American studios was . . . determined by the
class of audience they targeted."
```

Ellipses are not needed at the very beginning or end of a sentence. If the ellipsis ends a sentence in the middle of a quoted passage, include three periods for the ellipsis and a fourth for the period that ends the sentence.

2. Do not use quoted passages to make your points for you or to take up large blocks of space. Use them to support your points.

3. If you are quoting a long piece of dialogue from the movie or an exchange between two characters, this is usually double-spaced and indented rather than put in quotation marks in your text:

```
Bernard: First of all, not all women. And second-
         ly you frightened me. Sometimes you
         looked at me severely, and even with a
         certain hostility.
Marion: With a certain hostility? Really?
```

Passages longer than four lines of typescript should also be indented, without quotation marks. When you indent to quote dialogue or long passages, triple-space before and after the quote and either single-space or double-space the passage, depending on the preference of your instructor. Most publications ask that these passages be double-spaced like the rest of the manuscript, but for most student research papers, a single-spaced passage looks better.

4. Introduce your quotations; never end one sentence and begin the next with an unannounced quotation. Most commonly, this means acknowledging the speaker or the source of the passage with a phrase such as "André Bazin comments:" or "As Kracauer has argued in *Theory of Film* . . . ." For quotations that are especially important to your argument, or that may be a bit difficult to relate to your point, a nearby phrase or sentence can rephrase the central point so that it is not missed: "The debate about the relation of the film image and physical reality becomes an explicitly social issue in the work of André Bazin. As he says . . . ."

5. When integrating quotations into your own sentences, make them as succinct as possible and adjust them to fit the grammar and syntax of your prose. At times you may wish to use brackets in order to insert your own language into the middle of a quote (as in No. 1 above).

6. In American usage, periods and commas are placed inside the quotation marks, colons and semicolons outside. Exclamation points, question marks, and dashes are placed inside the quotation marks when they are part of the original passage, outside when they are part of your sentence.

7. When there is a quotation within the quote you are using, use single quotation marks for the inner quotation:

   `"The most provocative and problematic statement in`

   `Kracauer's work is `the redemption of physical`

   `reality.'"`

   If this embedded quotation were part of an indented passage, it would appear with double quotation marks because the block of indented sentences is not enclosed within quotation marks.

8. Double quotation marks are used to set off the titles of shorter works such as essays, articles, short poems, and songs. Underline titles of movies, books, long poems, album titles, plays, and paintings. Whether a movie is short or long, its title is underlined (or, when set in type, italicized). Song titles within the film are in quotation marks. The title of a screenplay is underlined.

The titles of television shows are underlined; episodes of those shows appear in quotation marks.

ACKNOWLEDGING SOURCES

When writing an essay, you must maintain a clear sense of what is your own thinking and what you have borrowed from others. Acknowledging and noting other perceptions and comments never diminishes the quality or strength of your paper; on the contrary, those acknowledgments strengthen and legitimize your ideas by placing them in the context of other work. Problems arise when, for one reason or another, a reader believes you are not making a clear distinction between your own perceptions and ideas and someone else's. In those instances, the trust between a reader and a writer is broken, and, at the very least, a reader will begin to doubt that the writer truly understands what he or she is saying. A suspicion of plagiarism can undermine all the hard work that has gone into a paper. Consequently, when researching and writing, you must maintain a sure distinction between sentences and words taken directly from another source, paraphrases or summaries of someone else's words, and general ideas appropriated from another source.

Taking the following passage as source material, let's consider the requirements and strategies for using and acknowledging secondary sources.

> The Neorealists were working for a cinema intimately connected with the experience of living: nonprofessional actors, rough technique, political point, ideas rather than entertainment — all these elements went directly counter to the Hollywood esthetic of smooth, seamless professionalism. While Neorealism as a movement lasted only until the early fifties, the effects of its esthetics are still being felt. In fact, Zavattini, Rossellini, De Sica, and Visconti defined the ground rules that would operate for the next thirty years. Esthetically, Hollywood never quite recovered. (Monaco 253)

1. Direct quotation. Phrases from this passage or the entire passage may be taken as needed to make your point. You will introduce the phrases or sentences, place the precise wording within quotation marks, and place the proper references to the work (usually author's name and page number) in parentheses:

Neorealism was not simply a localized and shortlived phenomenon. As James Monaco puts it, "While Neorealism as a movement lasted only until the early fifties, the effects of its esthetics are still being felt. In fact, Zavattini, Rossellini, De Sica, and Visconti defined the ground rules that would operate for the next thirty years. Esthetically, Hollywood never quite recovered" (253).

The exact form you use when citing the source for a quotation can differ (see pp. 161–163), but some acknowledgment should be made following a direct quotation.

2. Paraphrasing or summarizing information. The specific wording of a passage may be less important than the central conceit, which a writer might then wish to paraphrase or summarize. To paraphrase from another writer's work means to rephrase sentences so that they fit your prose better; to summarize usually suggests a reduction of the original passage, which nonetheless retains the core of the meaning in the new words. Unless the author writes badly, it is usually better to summarize than to paraphrase. In either case, proper credit must be given to the original source:

In How To Read a Film, James Monaco points out that Italian Neorealists were concerned with living experience, and shared basic tenets about filmmaking: nonprofessional actors, an emphasis on ideas and politics, and an unglossy look quite unlike Hollywood's. Especially through the work of individuals like Zavattini, Rossellini, De Sica, and Visconti, the effects of Neorealism were felt for three decades after its first appearance in the late forties, and to some

```
extent Hollywood has never totally recovered from
its aesthetic impact (253).
```

3. Acknowledging an idea. Sometimes a writer borrows an idea to use in such a general or brief manner that it is unnecessary to quote the original or even to paraphrase or summarize it. If you determine that the idea is original enough that the source deserves mention, be certain to do that. If you are in doubt, it is better to acknowledge a source than to risk a charge of plagiarism. In an essay on the Hollywood realism of the sixties, for instance, a writer might note in passing: "Although many consider Hollywood a fairly enclosed world, Neorealism had, as James Monaco has suggested, a definite effect on the Hollywood productions that followed it." No more formal citation is necessary, except for the listing of Monaco's book in the "Works Cited" section of your paper; yet general acknowledgments such as these prevent any confusion on the part of your reader and often lend authority to your own argument.

Note: The information or dialogue you take from a film usually does not need formal acknowledgment as long as you clearly refer to the title of the film that the information comes from. However, when you use a script, you should acknowledge and document that source. Finally, when you know that there is more than one version of a film circulating — as with *The Man Who Fell to Earth* (1976) or *M* — it is a good idea to specify which version you are using.

Common Knowledge

As you continue to read about, discuss, and write about the movies, you will realize that what you once took for an original idea or insight seems more like common knowledge. This is a consequence of your growing understanding of the field. Thus, at first you might be inclined to quote or cite an article that remarks that "Italian Neorealism, for all practical purposes, began in 1945 with Rossellini's *Open City.*" But as you grow more familiar with film and film literature, you realize that this information is standard, can be found in many sources, and does not require attribution. Using it in a later paper, you might decide that there is no need for a formal acknowledgment.

The status of information does change. When a statement first appears it may be a fairly original proposition; as it becomes assimilated into the critical literature, it gradually becomes common knowledge. There will be judgment calls, when you have to decide whether the information is or is not common knowledge. In the passage by James Monaco, a well-read writer would no doubt find it unnecessary to quote or refer to Monaco if he or she noted that Neorealism used unprofessional actors, had an unpolished look, or was based on political commitment. A less well-read writer may feel insecure without making some mention of the source where the statement was first discovered. Again, follow a simple guideline: when in doubt about whether to cite and document a source, do it.

DOCUMENTING SOURCES

Documenting your sources can be a confusing business because there are so many formats for documentation. The British, for instance, have traditionally used a slightly different system of punctuation and documentation; in the United States, there have always been a variety of styles and formats to choose from when doing notes. In any given collection of essays or books, one could find an MLA style or a Chicago style, footnotes or endnotes. Although you should ask your instructor whether there is a preferred style, the following is based on the MLA system of documentation and is acceptable in almost all situations.

Two kinds of notes can figure in an essay or a book:

1. Notes that document the source from which a quoted phrase or an idea comes
2. Notes that provide a commentary on some portion of your text or on a quotation you use

Notes for Documentation

In some formats, the writer can document with either footnotes or endnotes, but in the MLA format, only with commentary notes does the writer have that option. Notes used to document a source now always have a two-part structure: a reference within your text and a list of works cited that completes the documentation at the end of your essay. With notes of this kind, there is no longer a need to number your references. Instead, whenever there is explicit or implicit use of another source, use one of the following methods to acknowledge a source:

1. Cite the author's last name and the page numbers in parentheses at the end of your sentence:

```
A recent study has described these stunning
images in Ozu's films as "pillow shots" (Burch
160-161).
```

2. When you use the author's last name in your sentence, use only the page number or numbers of the source in your parentheses:

```
Noël Burch has described these stunning images in
Ozu's films as "pillow shots" (160-161).
```

3. When you are making a general reference to the work of an author whose name is mentioned in your sentence — rather than a specific reference — omit any parenthetical reference and document the source only in the list of Works Cited:

```
In a study of Japanese cinema for the period
1896-1933, Noël Burch examines the specific
discourses of the films and argues convincingly
for the distinctive excellence of the early films
of Ozu Mizoguchi and less well-known masters.
```

Although this reference is brief and general, it is not complete unless the entire reference to Burch's book is given in the "Works Cited" list.

Note that when the author's name and page number are included, no punctuation is necessary between the two. Normally, the parenthesis comes at the end of the sentence and is followed by a period. Only occasionally will you wish to insert the reference at the end of a clause, where it should be followed by a comma:

```
Although one commentator has argued convincingly
for a kind of "pillow shot" in Ozu's films (Burch
```

160-161), others have debated this designation.

When the reference is a long, indented passage, the parenthetical reference comes after the period at the end of the passage:

Less concerned with formal innovations, two other critics have praised the later Ozu films and locate their power in their perspectives on the family structure:

> In every Ozu film the whole world exists in one family. The ends of the earth are no more distant than outside the house. The people are members of a family rather than members of a society, though the family may be in disruption, as in Tokyo Story, may be nearly extinct, as in Late Spring or Tokyo Twilight, or may be a kind of family substitute, the small group in a large company, as in Early Spring. (Anderson and Richie 359)

There will be variations on these formulas. If your essay includes references to more than one work by the same author, you must be sure to indicate the title of the appropriate work in your text citation: (Burch, *Theory of Film Practice* 76). Likewise, if you use authors with the same last name, be certain to give first names or initials in any reference to them. When citing a work written by more than one author, include each name; if there are more than three authors, use the first name followed by "et al." For books with more than one volume, place the volume number and a colon after the author's name in the parentheses: (Roud 2: 991).

Works Cited

The list of Works Cited that appears at the end of your essay gives complete documentation of works you refer to in any way. Unless your instructor requests it, do not include books or articles that you consulted but did not use. If necessary, you can follow "Works Cited" with "Works

Consulted." These lists should each begin on a new page following your text or endnotes, and the pagination should continue in the same order.

The title "Works Cited" should be centered at the top of the page (without quotation marks and not underlined). The composition of this list is much like that of a traditional bibliography: last names first, alphabetical order, first line flush with the margin and turnover lines indented five spaces; double space between entries, and so on. Here, however, are a few other guidelines for the MLA format:

- When you list more than one work by the same author, alphabetize the works by title (ignoring initial articles such as "The"). Rather than repeat the author's name after the first entry, use three hyphens where the name would appear.
- Use shortened or abbreviated forms whenever possible: "PA" instead of "Pennsylvania"; "Little, Brown" instead of "Little, Brown and Company."
- Do not use a comma between a journal title and a volume number:

   `Film Quarterly 31.2`

- Do not use "p" or "pp" to indicate page numbers.
- For periodical articles, use a colon to separate the volume and year of publication from the specific page numbers:

   `Film Quarterly 37.4 (1984):6-18.`

- Use lowercase abbreviations to identify the roles of named writers (such as ed. for editor, trans. for translator). When these designations follow a period, capitalize the abbreviations.

The following are examples of typical entries in "Works Cited":

- A book with one author:

   `Everson, William K. American Silent Film. New`
   `     York: Oxford UP, 1978.`

- Two or more books by the same author:

   `Andrew, J. Dudley. Concepts in Film Theory. New`
   `     York: Oxford UP, 1984.`

--- The Major Film Theories. New York: Oxford UP, 1976.

- A book by two or more authors:

Talbot, David, and Barbara Zheutlin. Creative Differences: Profiles of Hollywood Dissidents. Boston: South End Press, 1978.

- An edited book:

Corrigan, Timothy, ed. The Films of Werner Herzog: Between Mirage and History. New York and London: Methuen, 1986.

- A book with an author and an editor:

Burch, Noël. To the Distant Observer: Form and Meaning in the Japanese Cinema. Ed. Annette Michelson. Berkeley and Los Angeles: Univ. of California Press, 1981.

- A work in an anthology:

Johnston, Claire. "Women's Cinema as Counter-Cinema." Movies and Methods. Ed. Bill Nichols. Berkeley and Los Angeles: Univ. of California Press, 1976. 208-217.

- A book that has been translated:

Burch, Noël. Theory of Film Practice. Trans. Helen R. Lane. Princeton: Princeton UP, 1981.

- A book with more than one volume:

Agee, James. Agee on Film. 2 vols. New York: Grosset & Dunlap, 1958.

- An article in a journal with continuous pagination:

```
Brustein, Robert. "Film Chronicles: Reflections
     on Horror Movies." Partisan Review 25
     (1958):291.
```

- An article in a journal that pages each issue separately:

```
Petro, Patrice. "Mass Culture and the Feminine:
     The 'Place' of Television in Film Studies."
     Cinema Journal 25.3 (1986):5-21.
```

It is unnecessary in the *Partisan Review* citation to indicate an issue number because, with continuous pagination, the volume number alone will suffice; in the *Cinema Journal* citation the issue number appears after the decimal point following the volume number. In the example that follows, both volume and issue numbers are omitted.

- Reviews and articles from periodicals or newspapers:

```
Sarris, Andrew. "Stranded in Soho's Mean Streets."
     The Village Voice 17 Sept. 1985:54.
```

- Interviews:

```
Kurosawa, Akira. Interview. "Making Films for All
     the People." With Kyoko Hirano. Cineaste
     14.4 (1986):23-25.
```

Notes Supplying Additional Commentary

A writer may wish to include an endnote or a footnote not to document a passage but to explain or comment on it further. Unless the note appears as a footnote at the bottom of the appropriate page, this type of note should appear on a separate page, numbered consecutively, and placed between the end of your text and the "Works Cited" page. The heading of the page, centered at the top, should be "Notes" or "Endnotes." The notes should begin five spaces in from the left margin. Numbers corresponding to the numbers in your text should be elevated half a line. When the note runs more than one line long, subsequent lines should begin flush with the margin. Double-space these notes, begin them with a capital letter, and end them with a period.

In general, there are two kinds of endnotes or footnotes: (a) one that supplies additional commentary on a point or a remark made in your text; and (b) one that refers readers to additional sources:

> `Before 1917, Russian film culture was mainly Euro-`
> `pean.`[1]

> `(a)`
>
> [1]`Although this statement is accepted by most film`
> `historians, recent scholarship suggests that there`
> `were other, more indigenous, film cultures beginning`
> `to appear in Russia well before 1917.`
>
> `(b)`
>
> [1]`For details and debate about early Russian film`
> `culture, see Leyda 3-90 and Taylor 1-20.`

Notice that the references and page numbers in the second note are cited in the standard fashion. Those references must then be documented in the list of works cited:

> `Leyda, Jay.` `Kino.` `3rd ed. Princeton: Princeton`
> `UP, 1983.`
> `Taylor, Richard.` `The Politics of Soviet Cinema`
> `1917-1929.` `New York: Cambridge UP, 1979.`

COMMON CONVENTIONS OF USAGE

We are all prone to common errors that may require special attention when composing and revising. Some students continually confuse "its" and "it's" (the first a possessive pronoun, like ours or his; the second a contraction for "it is"). Others have difficulty with subject-verb agreements, and they must regularly look out for this kind of mistake.

Commas, dashes, and hyphens can become crutches for a writer who is unsure how they can be used to divide or balance sentences and words. These are not trivial concerns in writing, whatever the subject, and every writer must become aware of chronic problems with usage that can be corrected. The following section reviews the most typical errors in writing about film.

Names

Always verify the spelling of the names of filmmakers, movie personnel, characters, and actors. Names can have difficult foreign spellings, and care must be taken to get them right. Some names might be accented or hyphenated, and when common usage indicates that initials are used for a first name (such as D. W. Griffith), that usage should be adhered to. In most instances, titles like Mr., Miss, or Ms. are dropped, and once a full name has been introduced in an essay, subsequent references usually use only the last name. Never use a first name alone to feign a casual stance toward a character or an actor.

Titles

Full titles of books and films, capitalized and underlined, should be given when they are first cited; after that, a writer can employ a common abbreviation: The *Apprenticeship of Duddy Kravitz* (1974) becomes just *Duddy Kravitz*. Frequently the shortened form becomes the traditional usage (Kubrick's *2001*), when the full title carries important information (*2001: A Space Odyssey*).

Whether to use the original foreign-language title or its English translation depends, to some extent, on your instructor. For film courses in foreign language departments, the original titles will probably be expected; in other courses, the English title will probably suffice. With some titles — *Viridiana* (1961), *Ballet Mécanique* (1924) — the original is also used in English. In some instances the English title used might have nothing to do with the original foreign title: Wim Wenders's *Im Lauf der Zeit* (1976) is literally translated as *In the Course of Time,* but the title of the film as released for American distribution is *Kings of the Road*. The best strategy here is to use both titles when you first refer to the movie: *Im Lauf der Zeit (Kings of the Road)*. Then, throughout the rest of the essay, use one version consistently.

Checking the accuracy of these titles can not only make for a more professional paper, but sometimes, as with the last example, suggest central themes that are lost in the translation. With some movies, the history of a title change can be the beginning of the essay itself: Ivan Passer's *Cutter's Way* (1981) went through several title changes before it achieved its modest success, and the history of those changes provides an interesting example of American distribution games.

Foreign Words and Quotation Marks

Perhaps because of its international mobility and scope, film has attracted a large number of terms and expressions from other languages, especially French. Words and phrases like "montage," "cinema verité," and "mise-en-scène" have become a standard part of the film vocabulary in English and can be found in recent English dictionaries. They accordingly do not necessarily need to be underlined or placed in quotation marks. In instances where less familiar terms are borrowed from a foreign language (such as the Japanese *benshi,* which refers to the person who narrated silent movies in that country), these words should be underlined to indicate italics.

When you quote dialogue or commentary in a foreign language, do not underline it. If there is any doubt about whether your reader or readers will know that language, you should append a translation in parentheses or in a footnote.

Sexist Language

When you are referring to a person or persons whose gender is unspecified, it can be offensive to presume and use a masculine pronoun ("Watching this movie, a modern spectator sees his world from a very different angle"). It is preferable to double or split those pronouns ("his or her"; "s/he"). But because this wording is awkward, it may be better yet to solve the problem by using the plural ("Watching this movie, modern spectators see their world from a very different angle") or by eliminating the possessive ("Watching this movie, a modern spectator sees the world from a very different angle"). When a gender difference involves nouns, a writer may use words that are not gender specific: instead of "man" or "mankind," use "person," "individual," or "people."

Spelling

Misspelling a director's name or the title of a film under discussion is a good way to undermine your paper from the beginning, since it implies a careless attitude toward the project. The spelling of certain words traditionally is a problem for many writers: for example, "parallel," "separate," "subtly," "symmetry," and "prominent." All of us have our own list of problem words that demand watching. Unhappily, there are no easy solutions for those who have difficulty with spelling, except perhaps being alert and attentive to it: a good writer always has a dictionary nearby and uses it.

LAST WORDS

My hope is that reading this book becomes a guide and a preparation. In those moments of inevitable frustration, recall the words of Racine: "My tragedy is finished. All that is left to do is to write it."

Appendix
Symbols Commonly Used in Marking Papers

All instructors have their own techniques for annotating essays, but many instructors make substantial use of the following symbols.

ab	faulty or undesirable abbreviation
agr	faulty agreement between subject and verb or betwen pronoun and antecedent
apos	apostrophe
awk(k)	awkward
cap	use a capital letter
cf	comma fault
choppy	too many short sentences—subordinate
cl	cliché

coh	paragraph lacks coherence, sentence lacks coherence
cs	comma splice
dev	paragraph poorly developed
dm	dangling modifier
emph	emphasis obscured
good	a good point; or, well expressed
frag	fragmentary sentence
id	unidiomatic expression
ital	underline to indicate italics
k (awk)	awkward
l	logic; this does not follow
lc	use lower case, not a capital
mar	margins
mm	misplaced or dangling modifier
¶	new paragraph
paral	faulty parallel; or, use a parallel here
pass	weak use of the passive
ref	reference of pronoun vague or misleading
rep	undesirable repetition

run	run–on sentence
series?	false series
source	give your source
sp	misspelling
sub	subordinate
t	tense incorrect
trans	transition needed
u	lack of unity
usage	faulty usage
wordy	
ww	wrong word
X	this is wrong
?	really? are you sure? I doubt it; or, I can't read your writing

GLOSSARY

This guide to the most commonly used terms and concepts discussed in this book consists of a list of **Film Terms**, those having to do with cinema studies, followed by a list of **Writing Terms**, those having to do with writing strategies. Several good film glossaries are available as single texts, such as John Mercer's *Glossary of Film Terms* (University Film Assoc. Monograph No. 2, Summer 1978).

FILM TERMS

angle The position of the camera or point of view in relation to the subject being shown. Seen from above, the subject would be shot from a "high angle"; from below, it would be depicted from a "low angle."

close-up An image in which the distance between the subject and the point of view is very short, as in a "close-up of a person's face."

composition The arrangement and relationship of the visual elements within the frame of the image.

continuity editing An editing style which follows a linear and chronological movement forward, as if the image were simply recording the action. Because it creates the illusion of realism, it is often called "invisible editing."

crane shot An image depicting the subject from overhead, usually shot with a camera mounted on a mechanical crane.

cutting Changing from one image to another; this linkage is sometimes referred to as "montage."

eyeline match The editing or joining of shots by following the logic and direction of a character's glance or look.

formalism A critical perspective that mainly attends to the structure and style of a movie or group of movies.

frame The borders of the image within which the subject is composed.

genre A critical category for organizing films according to shared themes, styles, and narrative structures; examples are horror films and gangster films.

ideology An analytical approach that attempts to unmask the stated or unstated social and personal values that inform a movie or a group of movies.

long shot An image in which the distance between the camera and the subject is great, as in a "long shot of a distant ship."

mise-en-scène The arrangement of the so-called theatrical elements before they are filmed; they include lighting, costumes, and props.

narrative The way a story is constructed through a particular point of view and arrangement of events.

point of view The position from which an action or a subject is seen, often determining its significance.

scene A space within which a narrative action takes place; it can be composed of one or more shots.

sequence A series of scenes or shots unified by a shared action or motif.

shot A continuously exposed and unedited image of any length.

sound effects Any number of uses of sound other than music or dialogue.

take The recording of an image on film, usually used in writing as a temporal measure, such as a "long take" or a "short take."

tracking shot The movement of the image through a scene, photographed by a camera mounted on tracks. A dolly shot creates the same movement with a camera mounted on a mechanical cart, while a hand-held camera is mounted on a cameraperson's shoulder.

voice-over The voice of someone not seen in the narrative image who describes or comments on that image.

zoom shot The movement of the image according to focal adjustments of the lens without moving the camera.

Writing Terms

coherence The maintenance of a single idea or thought in order to keep a sentence, paragraph, or essay focused and logical.

concluding paragraph A final paragraph of an essay which may recall earlier arguments and/or suggest new arguments related to the essay.

connotation The cultural or suggested meanings of a word.

denotation The literal meaning of a word.

essay Most frequently, a specific description of and argument about a particular subject.

film theory The larger methods and approaches that can inform the way a writer looks at, thinks about, and writes about the movies, such as a feminist or historical point of view.

outline The blueprint for an argument that insures a clear and logical organization of major and minor points.

paraphrasing Translating the words or ideas of someone else into the writer's own words; the original source still needs to be acknowledged.

proofreading The crucial rereading of the final draft of an essay in order to correct for misspellings, grammatical errors, and other problems.

review A short piece of writing that introduces a movie in general terms by describing its story and evaluating its achievements.

topic sentence Usually the first sentence of a paragraph; it states clearly the idea that organizes that paragraph.

thesis paragraph The first paragraph of an essay, which announces the subject (such as a particular film or topic) and then focuses the topic on a more exact argument.

thesis statement Perhaps the single most important part of a critical essay, clearly and precisely stating the direction and main points of the argument that will follow; most often it appears at the end of the first paragraph.

transitions The words and phrases that link one paragraph to another and one sentence to another.

WORKS CITED

Allen, Robert, and Douglas Gomery. *Film History: Theory and Practice.* New York: Knopf, 1985.

Altman, Rick. "The Evolution of Sound Technology." *Film Sound: Theory and Practice.* Ed. Elisabeth Weiss and John Belton. New York: Columbia Univ. Press, 1985. 44-53.

Anderson, Joseph, and Donald Richie. *The Japanese Film: Art and Industry.* New York: Grove, 1969.

Andrew, Dudley. *Film in the Aura of Art.* Princeton: Princeton Univ. Press, 1984.

Barnet, Sylvan. *A Short Guide to Writing about Literature.* Boston: Little, Brown, 1985.

Barr, Charles. "CinemaScope: Before and After." *Film Quarterly* 16.4 (1963): 4-25.

Barsam, Richard Mersam. "Leni Riefenstahl: Artifice and Truth in a World Apart." *Film Comment* 9 (1973): 32-37.

Barthes, Roland. "The Face of Garbo." In *Mythologies.* Trans. Annette Lauers. New York: Farrar, Straus & Giroux, 1972.

Bazin, André. *What Is Cinema?* Vol. 2. Trans. Hugh Gray. Los Angeles: Univ. of California Press, 1971.

Bordwell, David, and Kristin Thompson. *Film Art: An Introduction.* 2nd ed. New York: Knopf, 1986.

Canby, Vincent. "The Screen: *Badlands* Is Ferociously American." *The New York Times* 24 March 1974: 40.

Clair, René. "The Art of Sound." *Film Sound: Theory and Practice.* Ed. Elisabeth Weiss and John Belton. New York: Columbia Univ. Press, 1985. 92-95.

Cook, David. *A History of Narrative Film.* New York: Norton, 1981.

De Lauretis, Teresa. *Alice Doesn't: Feminism, Semiotics, and Cinema*. Bloomington: Indiana Univ. Press, 1984.

Elsaesser, Thomas. "*Shock Corridor* by Samuel Fuller." *Movies and Methods*. Vol. 1. Ed. Bill Nichols. Los Angeles: Univ. of California Press, 1976. 290-296.

Hendersen, Brian. "Exploring *Badlands*." *Wide Angle* 5.4 (1983): 38-55.

Hess, John. "*Godfather II*: A Deal Coppola Couldn't Refuse." *Jump Cut* 7 (1975): 10-11.

Langer, Susanne. *Feeling and Form*. New York: Scribners, 1953.

Liehm, Mira. *Passion and Defiance: Film in Italy from 1942 to the Present*. Los Angeles: Univ. of California Press, 1984.

Mast, Gerald. *Howard Hawks, Storyteller*. New York: Oxford Univ. Press, 1982.

Monaco, James. *How To Read a Film*. New York: Oxford Univ. Press, 1981.

Nicoll, Allardyce. "Film Reality: The Cinema and the Theater." *Film: An Anthology*. Ed. Daniel Talbot. Los Angeles: Univ. of California Press, 1959. 33-50.

Nowell-Smith, Geoffrey. "Shape and a Black Point." *Sight & Sound* 33.1 [Quoted from *Movies and Methods*. Vol. 1. Ed. Bill Nichols. Los Angeles: Univ. of California Press, 1976. 354-362.]

Salt, Barry. *Film Style and Technology: History and Analysis*. London: Starwood, 1983.

Sklar, Robert. *Movie-Made America: A Cultural History of American Movies*. New York: Vintage, 1975.

Spoto, Donald. *The Art of Alfred Hitchcock*. New York: Doubleday, 1976.

Vogel, Amos. "On Seeing a Mirage." *Film Comment* 17.1 (1981): 76-78.

Warshow, Robert. *The Immediate Experience*. New York: Atheneum, 1975.

Wood, Robin. "Sam Peckinpah." *Cinema: A Critical Dictionary*. Vol. 2. Ed. Richard Roud. London: Martin Secker & Warburg, 1980. 771-775.

Credits

Index